"*50 Mindful Steps to Self-Esteem* is a wonderful and accessible book. Janetti Marotta speaks on the heart of the matter in helping us experience greater wisdom and compassion. This book is a gift!"

—**Bob Stahl, PhD**, coauthor of A Mindfulness-Based Stress Reduction Workbook, Living with Your Heart Wide Open, and Calming the Rush of Panic

"With evident simplicity, Janetti Marotta explores the paradox of self-esteem using a Buddhist perspective. Your heart will be lifted!"

—**Gregory Sims, PhD**, author of *Treating Spiritual Disorders* and cofounder of the American Psychological Association (APA) Division of Peace Psychology

"Those wanting to experience greater self-esteem and overall well-being will find this book invaluable. A big thank you to Janetti Marotta for capturing so clearly these timeless mindfulness teachings and practices. They have the potential of transforming the life of anyone who incorporates them as a lifestyle."

—**Sharon Allen,** senior mindfulness teacher at Insight Meditation South Bay

"Beautifully designed and written, easy to follow, and eminently practical. Let *50 Mindful Steps to Self-Esteem* serve as your hands-on toolbox for cultivating self-esteem."

—**Adrienne Samuels, PhD**
It Was MSG

"Janetti Marotta has gathered together a treasure trove of practical tools useful for anyone embarking on the development of mindfulness and self-discovery."

—**Shaila Catherine**, author of *Focused and Fearless: A Meditator's Guide to States of Deep Joy, Calm, and Clarity*

"If you would like to meet someone truly worthy of your love, who has unlimited reservoirs of loving kindness and compassion to give you in return and who will never leave you as long as you are alive—these simple and sweet mindful steps will not fail you. Take your time, take these steps, and you will find the sweet lover you've always longed for in the least likely of places—in your own heart."

—**Steve Flowers, MS, MFT**, author of *The Mindful Path through Shyness* and coauthor of *Living with Your Heart Wide Open*

"What a wonderful, warm, compassionate read for those struggling to find self-acceptance. In *50 Mindful Steps to Self-Esteem*, Janetti Marotta has provided straight-forward direction for opening the heart to the essential nature of what it means to be human. Using the mindfulness teachings and exercises in this book, anyone can find their way to a sense of self that is whole and acceptable—as is. … Not only will I practice these steps myself, but I have already made plans to share this work with friends, family and clients alike. Thank you for this incredible guide to building self-esteem."

—**Robyn D. Walser, PhD**, coauthor of *Acceptance and Commitment Therapy for Post-Traumatic Stress Disorder*, *Learning ACT*, and *The Mindful Couple*; associate director at the National Center for PTSD Dissemination and Training Division; and associate clinical professor at University of California, Berkeley

"Many of today's health issues can be attributed to the stresses and anxieties of modern-day living. This book is enlightening and hones in on key insights to help improve one's well-being. Janetti Marotta's practical exercises help us all build a solid foundation based on ancient wisdom for living in a modern complex world."

—**Bernice A. Stein, MD**, physician of sports medicine and medical acupuncture

"Janetti Marotta has given us a well-written, heartfelt guide to mindfulness practices that enhance awareness and nurture self-esteem from the inside-out. I can enthusiastically recommend this book."

—**Daniel Mandelbaum, MD**, psychiatrist, Ukiah, CA

"Through *50 Mindful Steps to Self-Esteem*, Janetti Marotta gives readers the necessary tools to find the most fitting meditative practice for any frame of mind. The positive effects of mindfulness shape awareness for the present and give structure for future practices. This book is wonderful. What a joy to read!"

—**Robin Springer, LAc**, owner of Essential Wellness, San Francisco, CA

"Most people are quite knowledgeable and well-versed when it comes to talking negatively about themselves and their personal qualities. What they are not so often able to do is to speak about—or see—themselves in a positive light. This book provides fifty ways to improve your self-esteem and make what is difficult a bit easier. ... This book can benefit those who are seasoned, confident people already, or people who lack confidence in many aspects of their life."

—**Gina M. Biegel, MA, LMFT**, author of *The Stress Reduction Workbook for Teens* and founder of the Mindfulness-Based Stress Reduction Program for Teens (MBSR-T)

"What a wonderful book! I was initially enthralled by the interesting chapter titles, but as I began to read became incredibly impressed with the specific, easy-to-understand, and practical nature of the fifty chapters. Janetti Marotta brings such a wealth of personal clinical experience to her writing that she has been able to integrate multiple philosophies and ideas from the ages into an effective, comprehensive, how-to book for anyone looking to improve their life. Her analogies and suggestions are eminently doable and, just like her, overwhelmingly gentle. This is a book for anyone and everyone who is struggling with life issues or just wants to improve their life with simple, everyday actions."

—**G. David Adamson, MD**, director of Fertility Physicians of Northern California and the Fertility and Reproductive Health Institute, clinical professor at Stanford University School of Medicine, and associate clinical professor at U.C. San Francisco School of Medicine

50 MINDFUL STEPS TO SELF-ESTEEM

Everyday Practices for Cultivating
Self-Acceptance & Self-Compassion

JANETTI MAROTTA, PHD

New Harbinger Publications, Inc.

Publisher's Note

This publication is designed to provide accurate and authoritative information in regard to the subject matter covered. It is sold with the understanding that the publisher is not engaged in rendering psychological, financial, legal, or other professional services. If expert assistance or counseling is needed, the services of a competent professional should be sought.

Distributed in Canada by Raincoast Books

Copyright © 2013 by Janetti Marotta
New Harbinger Publications, Inc.
5674 Shattuck Avenue
Oakland, CA 94609
www.newharbinger.com

Cover design by Amy Shoup; Text design by Michele Waters-Kermes;
Acquired by Jess O'Brien; Edited by Will DeRooy

Library of Congress Cataloging-in-Publication Data

Marotta, Janetti.
  50 mindful steps to self-esteem : everyday practices for cultivating self-acceptance and self-compassion / Janetti Marotta, PhD.
     pages cm
  Includes bibliographical references.
  ISBN 978-1-60882-795-4 (pbk. : alk. paper) -- ISBN 978-1-60882-796-1 (pdf e-book) -- ISBN 978-1-60882-797-8 (epub) 1. Self-esteem. 2. Self-acceptance. I. Title. II. Title: Fifty mindful steps to self-esteem.
  BF697.5.S46M37 2013
  158.1--dc23
                                    2013037196

Printed in the United States of America

15   14   13

10   9   8   7   6   5   4   3   2   1   First printing

To my husband, Steve Woodward, for the
endless patience, encouragement, and space
he gave to make this project possible.

I love you.

CONTENTS

In Gratitude   ix

Introduction   1

The Foundation   8

The Journey   12

PART 1   Breathing and the Body   15
          1. A Deep, Full Breath   17
          2. Squeeze and Breathe   22
          3. Feel Every Loving Touch   24
          4. Turn Toward the Current   26
          5. In and Out   29
          6. An Embodied Practice   32
          7. Read the Inscription   35
          8. Explore Sensations Within   37
          9. Hold Court   41
          10. Integrate and Harmonize   45
          11. Flow with Energy   50
          12. Greet the Earth   53
          13. The Lesson of Seaweed   58

PART 2   Thinking and the Mind   61

          14. An Impartial Witness   63
          15. Stop the Sorting   66
          16. Don't Know   69
          17. See the Whole Elephant   72
          18. Eat As If It's the First Time   74
          19. Being vs. Doing   77
          20. Release the Grip   80
          21. Spin the Wheel of Paradox   84
          22. Let Go of Attachment   89
          23. Catch a Monkey   92
          24. Stop After the First Arrow   95
          25. Pain Times Resistance
              Equals Suffering   100
          26. Turn to Look   103
          27. Get to Know It   105
          28. No Blame   110
          29. The Unfolding Process   114
          30. The Buddha Within   117

PART 3   Emotions and the Heart   121
         31. Spaciousness   123
         32. The Forces of Mara   126
         33. Explore the Container   130
         34. A Place of Balance   133
         35. Interweave   137
         36. Tend and Befriend   140
         37. Plant Your Garden   145
         38. Well-Wishing   148
         39. Send and Receive   152
         40. What Am I Ignoring?   155
         41. Count Your Blessings   157
         42. Delight for Others   159
         43. Taste the Elixir   163
         44. An Antidote   165

PART 4   Being in the World   169
         45. Claim Your Emotional Baggage 171
         46. Listen—Just Listen   176
         47. Speak with Compassion   181
         48. Practice Nonharming   185
         49. Write Your Job Description   189
         50. Life Is the Practice   191

         Epilogue   195

         Resources   199

         References   201

IN GRATITUDE

The concept of a book that helps the reader nurture self-esteem through practices that cultivate self-acceptance and self-compassion grew out of a series of long discussions between me and my colleague Renée Burgard, LCSW. For her guidance and insight concerning the concept and structure of this book, I am extremely grateful. Her contributions included highlighting acceptance as the core mindfulness practice; using the seven attitudinal qualities of mindfulness; beginning with the foundational practices of breathing and the body; incorporating the writings of Thich Nhat Hanh; and using teaching stories.

Thanks to Jon Kabat-Zinn, PhD, who has brought the ancient practice of mindfulness into mainstream medicine through his mindfulness-based stress reduction (MBSR) program. His seven "pillars of mindfulness" inspired, informed, and enriched the practices for self-acceptance in this book.

Thanks to Kristin Neff, PhD, who has been a pioneer in opening up self-compassion as a field of study. She views self-compassion as the alternative to self-esteem, and most psychologists agree. In this book, self-compassion is central to nurturing mindful self-esteem, and is cultivated through practices based on seven Buddhist qualities linked to compassion.

Many of the teachings and practices in this book have also been inspired by influential teachers of the mindfulness community, including Jack Kornfield, Joseph Goldstein, Sharon Salzberg, Sylvia Boorstein, Phillip Moffitt, Tara Brach, and Gil Fronsdal. Additional influences include Daniel Siegel, Rick Hanson, Saki Santorelli, and Ronald Siegel. The perspectives of world-renowned masters, including Vietnamese Buddhist monk and Zen master Thich Nhat Hanh, American Buddhist nun Pema Chödrön, and His Holiness the Dalai Lama, bring a sense of poetry and the ineffable, as well as the clearest expressions of the heart of mindfulness teachings. To them and others held in "true esteem" from ancient times to the present day, I express gratitude.

I am fortunate to have been mentored by Bob Stahl, who started the spread of MBSR in Northern California through his MBSR teacher training program. My primary meditation teacher today is Shaila Catherine, founder and principal teacher of Insight Meditation South Bay (IMSB). I continue to bring mindfulness more fully into my life from her dharma talks and retreats.

I am indebted to acquisitions editor Jess O'Brien of New Harbinger Publications for his encouragement, perseverance, and belief in me as a writer. It was my particular good fortune to be paired with copyeditor Will DeRooy, whose impact on the book was no less than transformative. Thanks to New Harbinger Publications and the editorial team of Jess Beebe, Nicola Skidmore, Nelda Street, and Angela Autry Gorden for their helpful feedback and suggestions.

Appreciation to Leslie Woodward for early editorial assistance and to Bob Loftis, Nisar Shaikh, Trudy Roughgarden, and Edy Young for early readings. Thanks to David Adamson, MD, and my colleagues at Fertility Physicians of Northern California, whose mindfulness-based programs integrate many of the practices in this book.

I am extremely blessed to be part of an accepting and compassionate family, in particular my husband, Steve; my children, Prairie, Tenaya, and Cheyenne; my mother, Clara; and my siblings, Nancy, Liz, and Jeffrey. They and many others too numerous to name have provided great models of how, as Stephen Levine wrote, "the heart has room for everything" (1979, 70). This project is born from their love.

INTRODUCTION

Do you often feel inadequate, flawed, or imperfect? Do you frequently make critical, judgmental statements about yourself or find yourself wishing *If only I were thinner...*, *If only I were more successful...*, *If only I were smarter...*, *If only I were prettier...*, or *If only I had more money...*? Do you take everything that happens, including what others say and do, to mean something about you personally? Do you feel as if your worth depends on whether you succeed or fail—or on whether you're strong or weak? Do you tend to focus more on what's *wrong* with you than on what's *not* wrong? Do you habitually feel dissatisfied and discouraged because you aren't who you want to be? Do you often feel alone in your inadequacies?

This is the dilemma of self-esteem that we all share at times. It's easy to get caught in unrealistic expectations—expectations that can never be met—and look outside ourselves to "get it right" and be okay, believing that this is where we'll find what we need to prove our worth to ourselves. Our tendency is to compare how we're doing against others and wrap our identity around stories we tell about ourselves. All too often, these misguided efforts lead to feelings of unworthiness. It's probably this very inadequacy and insecurity that drew you to this book (and, for the most part, led me to write it).

50 Mindful Steps to Self-Esteem is intended to turn your thinking around and open your heart, so you can consider the possibility that what you've been looking for has actually been there all along!

Self-Esteem Seen Through the Lens of Mindfulness

We all struggle to accept what Buddha described as the three basic truths of our existence:

1. Life is difficult (*dukkha*).

2. Everything changes (*anicca*).

3. There is an ever-fluctuating flow of experience (*anatta*).

That is to say, we're dissatisfied when our lives aren't how we want them to be, we struggle against change, and we fight to hold on to a permanent sense of self. Basically, we can't control life, we have difficulty with this lack of control, and we take this inability personally. We don't want to feel inadequate or insecure, so we set about trying to re-create ourselves. We attempt to hold on to those parts of ourselves we like and get rid of those parts we dislike. We strive to lock in a permanent stamp of approval.

But when we deny certain parts of ourselves, it means we're not 100 percent available to ourselves or those we care about. When we constantly defend against failure and disapproval, it's as if we're carrying a heavy protective shell, unable to move about freely and do many things that are important to us in life.

When you learn to embrace all parts of yourself—accept yourself unconditionally—your inherent worth comes to the surface. You're open and, unburdened by your heavy defenses, you're able to truly be there for yourself and others. As you learn to accept the changing nature of all things, you know that both success and failure come and go. When you recognize that your life is an unfolding process, you sense a way of relating to yourself that lies beyond personal definition. From a Buddhist perspective, self-esteem can be defined as *self without definition*.

As you deeply connect with yourself, you recognize that you're already whole and complete as you are. By "befriending yourself" and cultivating qualities that invite wholeness, you open yourself up to whatever arises, with unconditional acceptance. In this unfolding process, you experience that your essential nature—your *Buddha nature*—is good and pure and that you're part of something even greater. You and the world are, in a sense, one.

From the *wakefulness* of awareness, the *warmth* of compassion, and the *wisdom* of the journey comes *connecting* to others, *caring* for a larger whole, and *committing* to your core values no matter what comes your way. Mindful self-esteem is an unfolding process that cultivates self-acceptance and self-compassion—qualities that offer strength, clarity, love, and commitment for being human on this journey we call life.

The "Presents" of Mindfulness

Mindfulness involves opening to the present moment just as it is, without trying to hold on to what you like about it or get rid of what you don't like. Part of mindfulness is thus "being with" yourself as you are, despite your desire to be otherwise. Your sense of self is not derived from your narrative story, which is fixed in time, but rather from your immediate experience, which is ever-changing. Being mindful is like being a kite let free to fly on the currents. Sometimes you soar high and fast; other times you turn circles and fall to the ground. The outcome isn't what matters. What matters is getting up and beginning again, letting go of the disappointment of crashing. It's not what happens, but *how you relate to* what happens, that makes all the difference. Mindfulness invites you to say yes to life, something that's especially helpful when you're easily discouraged and cling to notions of what you should or shouldn't be.

Mindfulness meets the weather of discontent as an opportunity for learning, for new growth. This brings an attitude of curiosity: paying attention in an open, friendly way. It reverses any tendency to run or hide and asks that you turn *toward* that which is difficult (rather than avoid it) and make space for it to be. Rather than saying, *I'm inadequate*, you say, *Ah, so this is what inadequacy feels like!* Mindfulness teaches that life is to be experienced through the senses, not through the mind's running commentary.

Mindfulness teaches you to live with what's happening right now, so you don't get caught up in guilt about the past or fear about the future. Your life isn't whatever's on your to-do list or the things you've done up to now; it's what's actually happening. Staying in the present shifts your focus from what's wrong to what's *not* wrong. You can imagine how freeing this is!

When you're mindful, you steer your life with intention. This fosters goodness when you vow to open yourself up to whatever comes your way and awaken to wisdom with the embrace of compassion. With *intention* comes *attention*—looking deeply into who you *really* are and what life is all about. This serves as a great resource, because it keeps you from getting mired in sticky thoughts or losing yourself in unimportant details.

Mindfulness takes you out of automatic patterns of behavior; rather than mindlessly reacting, you consciously respond in more productive ways. More than using thinking as a way out of challenging situations, mindfulness uses awareness as a way *through*. As Robert Kaplan (1999,

1) wrote, "If you look at zero you see nothing; but look through it and you will see the world."

Practices for Mindful Self-Esteem

A cornerstone of mindfulness is *acceptance*. Acceptance doesn't mean that everything is okay; it means recognizing things are as they are and reducing your resistance to them. Acceptance is a practice of getting curious—discovering what causes you to feel uncomfortable. It's the essential paradox of turning things around—moving toward that which you resist. In order to do this, you bring to bear the qualities of *nonjudging, nonstriving, beginner's mind, letting be,* and *patience.* These interrelated qualities, which will be fully discussed in part 2, build upon one another and culminate in a greater capacity for *trust as self-reliance*: being able to rely on your mind and body through deep connection. These qualities are the seven "pillars of mindfulness" identified by Jon Kabat-Zinn (1990, 31–41).

Another cornerstone is *compassion*. Compassion toward yourself infuses your awareness with warmth. Buddhist psychology recognizes compassion as an intrinsic quality of the mind, part of human nature. As you heal from the emotional scars of unworthiness, you're held in the warm embrace of the heart and are able to compassionately care for others. This compassionate awareness leads to increased openness, equanimity, loving-kindness, gratitude, sympathetic joy, and generosity.

Yet another cornerstone is living life with virtue, purpose, and intention for the greater good. This means honoring the sanctity of all living things, with an awareness that all are one and the same. It entails the recognition that you're not alone in your imperfection, and the willingness to embrace the challenge of being human. It's a commitment to base your actions on not causing harm to yourself or others. When you cultivate mindful self-esteem, the qualities of acceptance, compassion, and virtue live within you as inseparable triplets.

THE
FOUNDATION

How do you turn your attention from seeking conditional acceptance to cultivating unconditional acceptance and compassion? How do you reverse your need to gain others' approval, to cultivate your inner qualities and honor your inherent worth? How do you let go of a separate sense of self, limited by fear, to experience an expansive "field" of being?

The answer is you begin where you are. You're the only one who can plant the seed of mindful self-esteem.

By starting where you are, you can look inside to your unfolding process. You can get your judgmental thoughts out of the way, get into the present moment, and find that the person you've been looking for has been there all along. Waking up and loving yourself and others with intention is tending the seeds for mindful self-esteem!

About This Book

This book, *50 Mindful Steps to Self-Esteem*, consists primarily of simple, brief *mindfulness practices* for you to settle into each morning, perhaps before your customary cup of tea or coffee, and to sprinkle throughout your day—at work, at home, or wherever you may go. There are meditations to foster and deepen your awareness and compassion; journaling exercises for you to note which actions lead to feelings of positivity and which lead to feelings of negativity; and activities for you to play with and enjoy. By starting where you are, with a spirit of curiosity, you'll find that your moments of mindfulness lengthen and, over time, become a "way of being." As you travel through this book and cultivate qualities for mindful self-esteem, you'll be introduced to the formal practices of meditation—both in stillness and in movement—and the informal practices of applying mindfulness to everyday life as you pay attention, on purpose, to the present moment. The practices will train your mind to stay with your experience: not feel the need to do anything to change how you're feeling. You'll come to know yourself as you look deeply into your habitual reactions and not lose yourself in self-critiques, comparisons, and feelings of unworthiness; you'll come to know how things really are, not how you interpret them to be. You'll uncover your wholeness and your wisdom.

Through meditation, you'll use your breath, your body, and other things to focus your *attention*. By focusing your mind on your moment-to-moment experience, you'll learn how to "work with" what's actually present: apply neutral attention so you can turn toward that which you resist. You'll bring the *intention* of staying fully present to your meditation, so you can come to intimately know what you're attending to and how it naturally unfolds. This will loosen the hold of the idea that you must look outside yourself for a permanent sense of self to forever legitimize who you are.

If you find any of these exercises particularly helpful, especially the formal practices of meditation both in stillness and in movement, this can serve as a means to establish a formal mindfulness practice. You may return to those exercises over and over as part of your daily practice. Making an intention to visit this book regularly and engage in the activities will help you begin, support, and maintain this evolving and liberating process. It may also help to listen to audio versions of the activities in this book as part of your formal practice. We've made audio versions of several of the meditations in this book available for you to download: please visit www.newharbinger.com/27954 to find them.

Committing to the practices and "showing up" to do them consistently, even for five minutes, is more important th   ow long you engage in them. Before breakfast, when returning home from work or school, and when going to bed are all opportune occasions for meditation. These transitional times of day invite you to pause before getting lured into your to-do list and busy schedule. Once you've established a place to practice, you might sometimes feel your heart drawing you to this place.

Many of the exercises in this book suggest journaling: putting your thoughts on paper. Journaling allows you to slow down your thinking, step back, and gain perspective, clarity, self-knowledge, and emotional healing. You may wish to buy a blank notebook and keep it handy.

The practices in the book take just a few minutes—or as long as you would like them to take. Because the teachings and practices are presented sequentially (that is, later ones build upon earlier ones), there's great benefit in learning the foundational practices of breathing and body awareness first, followed by the practices that "work with" thoughts, emotions, and relationships. There's also value in any sequence you choose. Anything you can do *mindfully*, no matter how small, is the most important practice. After all, even with small steps you may reach great heights!

THE JOURNEY

Before my daughter was born through surrogacy, for six years I was on the roller-coaster ride of infertility. During that time, I went through five lost pregnancies, a failed in vitro fertilization (IVF) attempt, several IVF cycles with donor eggs, and a canceled adoption.

Over those years, my sense of self dwindled to a feeling of total inadequacy and failure. I participated in every healing activity that came my way: counseling, acupuncture (along with an acupuncture "exorcism"), vision quests in the wilderness, a Christian church and Buddhist *Zendo*, and finally a unified East-West path that became my "spiritual home." Through meditation, the spiritual community, a pilgrimage to India, and the teachings of this spiritual path, I was able to more fully grieve for our lost babies and release my guilt, fear, and anxiety. I came to realize that my old coping strategy of trying harder to succeed didn't relate to how the world worked and had only resulted in a greater sense of failure—I needed to let go of my judgmental thoughts and preconceived notions of how things should be and open myself up to what was happening before me. By being aware of my thoughts and feelings and not letting them define me, I was able to work from the inside, open myself up to all family-building options, and develop the inner qualities of patience, trust, and acceptance I needed for the long haul.

The path I was on eventually led me to mindfulness. Mindfulness has opened me in even deeper ways, continually encouraging me to welcome what is here, regardless. At every turn, I'm inevitably invited to let go as I witness the instinctual pull of wanting to hold on to parts of myself I like and get rid of parts I dislike. I notice my resistance and say, *Ah, here you are again, my mischievous comrade—I know you well!* Then mindfulness comes along and shows me the way forward.

In the spirit of turning toward yourself and toward that which is difficult, what brings *you* here, and what's *your* deep intention?

Start Your Journey

Take the next few moments to settle your body and quiet your mind. Feel yourself supported by the furniture or floor upon which you rest. Notice your breath, feeling the sensations it creates in your body. Relax your eyes, inviting them to close, imagining that you're seeing from your heart instead of through your eyes. Feel the beating of your heart and the flow of your breath. Imagine each breath opening, expanding, even lifting your heart. There's no limit to the depth and breadth of your heart.

As you notice feelings coming and going, shifting and morphing, see them simply as images on a movie screen. No need to judge them as right or wrong; no need to judge them as good or bad. These are just visions appearing and disappearing. When these pictures capture your attention so much that you're compelled to watch them, just come back to feeling the beating of your heart and the rhythm of your breath. In this quiet space, ask yourself, *What brings me here, right now?*

Explore the deep motivation, the intention that led you to this book. Allow the intention to find *you*. Before ending this inward exploration, acknowledge a strength within yourself that can further you on this journey. Then, whenever you're ready, slowly and gently open your eyes.

PART 1

BREATHING
AND THE BODY

The intention in this part of the book is to set the stage for cultivating qualities of self-acceptance and self-compassion through the beginning practices of mindfulness of the breath and mindfulness of the body. Mindfulness teaches that when the body is relaxed, the mind will follow.

As you learn to still your mind with breath and body awareness practices, you're able to be truly present rather than being caught in the warp of thoughts and woof of emotions. These perpetual ups and downs initiate the prime directive: protect and defend. But focusing on finding Band-Aids for your wounds creates a vulnerable sense of self. In trying to fix a broken sense of self, you become lost to who you truly are.

When you bring your attention to your breath and body, the present moment is here to be touched. You're able to connect to what's actually happening, not your reactive thoughts about what's happening. Only in the present moment can you find your strength, learn to grow, and choose how you wish to respond to the experience of being you.

1. A Deep, Full Breath

The breath is closely tied to survival and emotional well-being. When you're confronted by danger, your autonomic nervous system induces shallow, rapid chest breathing. This is part of the stress response, also known as your "fight, flight, or freeze" response, in which your physiological processes speed up so that you're ready to respond to threat in an instant. In this state, it's hard to think rationally, and your emotions take over. Rapid chest breathing is one of the body's ways of stepping on the gas pedal and revving the engine. This ancient mechanism enabled early humans to run from dangers such as saber-toothed tigers and is credited with saving us from extinction.

But the brain can't distinguish between what's life threatening and what's only emotionally threatening. Emotional threats are "demon" tigers—internal voices that evaluate and compare how you're doing and whether you're doing it well enough. For every real tiger behind the bush, there are far greater numbers of "demon" tigers at large!

When you constantly determine whether you're measuring up, this turns on your stress response because you either forget to breathe or hardly breathe. Your feelings of insecurity increase. In this vulnerable state, you tend to mindlessly react, and in doing so you lose your connection with yourself.

The autonomic nervous system also controls the relaxation response, or "rest and digest" response, and like the stress response, it too is modulated by the breath. Deep, abdominal breathing signals the body to slow down and relax. This enables you to reside in the present moment and proceed calmly and deliberately. Imagine that you're driving along when suddenly traffic starts to slow down. If chest breathing is like stepping on the gas pedal, forcing you to drive erratically to avoid an accident, abdominal breathing is like stepping on the brake pedal and staying in your own lane.

When you bring your conscious awareness to your breath, your breathing naturally falls into a slower, steadier, and deeper rhythm, placing your brain into a peaceful state. You're able to give yourself and others a break because there's no emergency.

While relaxation is not the goal of mindfulness, abdominal breathing sets the conditions for staying in the present moment because it quiets and calms your mind. You can then create a space to unhook from "doing" and relax into "being"—enabling you to be a "gatherer" of internal acceptance rather than a "hunter" for external validation.

TRY THIS

Part of the following exercise is an adaptation of a visualization exercise taught by mindfulness-based stress reduction (MBSR) teacher Mark Abramson. Lie comfortably on your back, and slowly close your eyes. Notice how your breathing occurs naturally, without even a thought of *making* it happen. Allow yourself to sink into the floor or furniture.

1.   Place one hand on your chest, the other on your belly. With your mind's eye, imagine a balloon behind your belly button gently filling with air as you inhale and emptying as you exhale. Invite your belly to relax.

2.   Without trying to control or force your breath in any way, allowing *it* to lead you, notice, perhaps, your breath slowing and deepening. When your breath deepens, lengthens, and slows, your belly gently rises and falls, expands and collapses. In this soft, rhythmic flow, notice, perhaps, whether your hand on your belly moves more than your hand on your chest does. This tells you whether your breath is traveling past your chest and moving the muscle of your diaphragm down, causing your belly to rise and fall. If there's no difference between the movement of your hands, no worries. Over time, as you follow your breath with relaxed

attention, your breath slows and deepens on its own into its natural state.

3. Gently lower your hands and arms to your sides. Now imagine that you're floating on an air mattress in the ocean on a warm, sunny day. Visualize riding the gentle ocean waves: as you inhale, your belly slowly rises, as you're carried up the slope of a wave. As you exhale, your belly slowly falls, as you ride down the other side of the wave.

4. As you breathe from your belly, envisioning riding a wave with each breath, take a few moments to note how you're feeling.

5. Imagine that the ocean is getting a little choppy. For a short while, allow your breath to move only into your chest, so your breath is short, shallow, and faster, matching the motion of these smaller, shorter, faster waves.

6. While you're engaged in chest breathing, take a few moments to mentally note your feelings.

7. Picture the waves returning to their former gentle, slow movements, as you invite your breath to slow and deepen. While you take abdominal breaths fully and freely, your belly lifts on the slope of the inhalation and lowers on the decline of the exhalation.

8. While you're breathing in this way, take a few moments to observe your feeling state. When you're ready to leave the ocean, slowly open your eyes.

Were you able to feel a difference between these two states? If not, there's no need for concern. Give more time to this exercise or come back to it again later.

2. Squeeze and Breathe

Breath work has been revered through the ages as potent medicine for calming the mind and body. When you consistently breathe from your belly, you change patterns in your nervous system and in your mind. Abdominal breathing creates a cascade of calming effects, influencing such vital functions as blood pressure, heart rate, and airways in the lungs.

Abdominal breathing creates a deep, rich flow of carbon dioxide on the out-breath and a deep, rich flow of oxygen on the in-breath. As you expel waste in the form of carbon dioxide, you breathe in renewal in the form of oxygen. Rich, oxygenated blood reaches every part of your body. You can initiate your relaxation response at any time—for example, when you find yourself rushing through the day or worrying late at night. Through breathing practices, progressive muscle relaxation, guided imagery, yoga, or meditation, to name a few, abdominal breathing can become the way you typically breathe. Whenever you're feeling vulnerable to outside influences, you can shift your attention to the natural healing force of your breath and return to your centered, strong self.

TRY THIS

The following exercise demonstrates the power of the breath. Lie comfortably on your back, and slowly close your eyes.

1. For thirty seconds, tense your entire body: your face and neck, torso and pelvis, arms and hands, legs and feet, squeezing as tightly as possible (but without excessive force) as you breathe from your chest quickly and shallowly.

2. Release your hold on your body and relax. Consider what you noticed as you did the previous step.

3. For thirty seconds, tense your whole body again, squeezing with similar intensity, but this time breathe from your belly slowly and deeply.

4. Release your hold and relax. Consider what you were aware of as you did the previous step.

What was the difference between tensing your body while breathing from your chest and tensing your body while breathing from your abdomen? Did you notice a difference in what you were thinking or feeling, both emotionally and physically? Did time seem to pass more quickly or more slowly? Did you get a sense of how you can release tension and feel calm through bringing your attention to your breath? Was there even a slight sense of the calming capacity of the breath?

3. Feel Every Loving Touch

Life begins with the first breath and ends with the last. When you "touch" your breath, you "touch" life. When you feel lost, you can count on your breath to take you home to yourself.

One way to remember to "touch" your breath is by using your sense of touch. Touch can be a means of strengthening the mind-body connection. The sense of touch is widely used in prayer (as with Christian rosary beads), in meditation (as with Hindu *mala* strands), and to bring about a sense of calm (as with Middle Eastern worry beads). Touching is an instinctual way to self-soothe. Think of how when you're injured, your hand automatically goes to where it hurts.

TRY THIS

Breath reminder practices are commonly used to shift attention to abdominal breathing throughout the day. For example, in her MBSR classes Renée Burgard teaches students to use Velcro dots as reminders to focus on their breath. The following is an informal practice that I call FELT, an acronym for Feel Every Loving Touch. This practice can help you maintain a sense of calm and prevent anxiety from taking over.

Get several pieces of felt (about five to ten) of any size, and cut them into any shapes you like. Perhaps make one round, another square, and another in the shape of a heart or star. Maybe draw a happy face on one or write "breathe" on another. Place some of your felt shapes in places where you spend a lot of time; for example, by your computer or in the kitchen. Put one in your purse or your coat pocket, to take with you wherever you go. Put some in places where you often feel anxious—for example, by the phone or in the car. You might choose to glue some in place and keep others loose. Both on a regular basis and when you're feeling stressed, hold or rub one of these pieces of felt. Engage your soothing sense of touch as you take two or three deep, long abdominal breaths. Come to know your breath as your caring friend.

4. Turn Toward the Current

Because the mind is often miles away from the body, Vietnamese Buddhist monk and Zen master Thich Nhat Hanh (1976, 15) explains, the "breath is the bridge" that connects the mind to the body. Bringing your attention to your breath halts the incessant chatter of your thoughts and your concern with self-esteem. When your mind is adrift somewhere in the past or the future—lost in regret or worry—you can use your breath as an anchor to your body and to the present moment.

The more distracted your mind, the more opportunities you have to practice returning to your breath, because it's the "coming back" that matters. By using your breath as a constant, you learn how to not be swept away by disaffirming thoughts, and how to smooth out the ups and downs of believing you "should" be like *this* and "shouldn't" be like *that*. As you learn to relax into your breath and trust your mind to stay put, you begin to unhook from your conditioned state of control and mistrust and to rest in awareness itself: a space that's empty of preferences and full of life.

Mindfulness is at the heart of Insight meditation, or Vipassana, and Insight meditation is central to Buddhism. There are different approaches to the teaching of mindfulness, but traditionally it starts with mindfulness of the breath. In meditation, the breath becomes the "object of awareness." Daniel Siegel, MD (2010, 32), pioneer of the field of interpersonal neurobiology, describes the ability to bring both *attention* to the breath and *intention* to be fully present during meditation as the capacity to aim and sustain attention with an "observant," "objective," "open stance." This keeps you from identifying with your "inner critic," allowing change to occur. Through this process, your mind becomes receptive and resilient, able to shift its approach and move toward that which is difficult. What you previously thought of as your identity, you come to realize, is only part of your experience.

TRY THIS

Sit in an upright, relaxed position, whether in a chair or cross-legged on a pillow, and gently close your eyes. Allow your body to be held and supported as you rest your weight and feel the contact of your body with the chair or pillow.

Notice your breath naturally occurring. Gently bring your attention to your breath, and bring your intention to be fully present for this practice. You may notice sensations related to breathing: your belly may inflate and deflate; your chest may rise and fall; or your whole body may subtly expand and contract. Perhaps you notice that your nostrils and upper lip feel cool when you breathe in and warm when you breathe out. Instead of moving your attention from one part of your body to another, maintain your focus wherever your breath feels the most organic, animated, or lively. Come into intimate contact with each and every breath, noticing how each breath is special in its own way. Observe the depth and duration of each breath; the space or pause between the in-breath and the out-breath; and how the out-breath is slightly longer than the in-breath. Pay attention to the qualities, feeling, and rhythm of your breath. As you sense your breath, turn toward it so you can open to the full experience. It may feel as if you're riding on the waves of your breath, floating on its current, being massaged by your breath, or dancing with it.

During this exercise, know that the mind naturally wanders. It's easy to get distracted and lose touch with what you're doing. When this happens, just make a mental note: *Thinking*. Then gently but firmly lead your mind back to your breath—feeling each unique and ever-present breath sensation. Know that the intimacy you're establishing with your object of attention—in this case, your breath—is a kind of closeness you're forming with yourself. By honoring your intention to keep coming back to the breath, you're cultivating such qualities of mindfulness as nonjudgment, nonstriving, and patience. When you're ready, open your eyes and end this meditation, but continue to stay mindful of your breath throughout your day.

5. In and Out

The interdependence between breath and life intimately ties each of us to the planet Earth. All living beings are connected by the air we share.

When you find gratitude in your breath, you connect to this life force and the good fortune of being alive. You see life as a miracle and embrace that which is "us." Though each of us is unique, we are interconnected. Breaking down the barriers between you and others frees you from the need to be in competition with them. The breath is part of our common humanity—our inherent connection to one another.

In affirmation practices, people tell themselves positive things to help themselves feel or believe these things more strongly. In mind-body breath affirmation practices to reduce stress and bring a sense of calm, people focus on certain words, phrases, or imagery while mindfully breathing in and out. Aspiration practices, found in the Buddhist tradition, are similar to affirmation practices, except instead of telling themselves something they don't necessarily feel or believe, people express intentions of well-being and a willingness to move closer to what they fear.

From a Buddhist perspective, everything we do begins with intention or aspiration. By incorporating the power, sweetness, and rhythm of words and verses into a breathing meditation, you can cross over from where you are in this moment to where you aspire to be. You can use any word, phrase, or mantra to express intentions you wish to nurture for your own personal aspiration practice. The following exercise gives an example.

TRY THIS

For the following five-minute meditation, find a comfortable position and gently close your eyes.

1. Feel your breath in your body. Observe how each breath is unique and at the same time how each breath is connected to the next, in a flow. Sense the life force of your breath and its connection to life.

2. Breathe in and say to yourself, *Connection*. Breathe out and say to yourself, *Gratitude*. For several slow, long breaths, open to the feeling of connection to the planet, and open to the sense of gratitude for life.

3. Breathe in and say to yourself, *Safe*. Breathe out and say to yourself, *Secure*. With each breath, allow the feeling of safety to arise, and allow the feeling of security to extend and expand.

4. Breathe in and say to yourself, *Wholeness*. Breathe out and say to yourself, *Completeness*. With every breath, sense the feeling of a whole and complete self, and touch upon your connection to everyone and all of life.

Savor these aspirations, and carry them into your day.

6. An Embodied Practice

A self-esteem based on external measurement affects not only your mind, but also the way you relate to your body. At one extreme, your attention may be toward body image, appearance, and sexual attraction; you may view your body as a commodity, to be manicured, styled, and dressed. At the other extreme, your body may be starved for attention; you may devalue appearance, diet, exercise, and sleep, with the result that your overall health and well-being fall to the wind.

The body is at the center of mindfulness. Buddha states: "If the body is not cultivated, the mind cannot be cultivated. If the body is cultivated then the mind can be cultivated" (Fronsdal 2001, 48). Mindfulness is under the umbrella of mind-body medicine and is considered an "embodied practice": it focuses attention on how the body responds to thoughts, emotions, and experiences.

Staying connected to your body grounds your attention and keeps your mind from spinning and colliding with itself. Rather than experiencing life in your head, through reactive thoughts and emotions, you allow it to enter through your body, enabling you to create distance from your thoughts and emotions and respond in a more conscious, relaxed way.

When you're bombarded by thoughts and overwhelmed by emotions—or, conversely, when you reject your thoughts and suppress your emotions, you disconnect from what's actually occurring, taking you in directions that are often not in your best interest. Have you ever noticed an impulse to eat when you feel "down," particularly when you've made a commitment to lose weight; or the urge to have a glass of wine when you feel stressed, even though you're aware of negative side effects? These kinds of unhealthy connections are linked to mind-body disconnections.

When you cultivate body awareness, your attention resides in the here and now, where you can participate in the experience of life. Bringing awareness to the body brings awareness to the mind. Once you start making connections between your body and your mind, when unpleasant feelings arise you might not automatically want to grab that box of cookies or that bottle of chardonnay. You might choose to go for a hike in the woods or meditate instead!

TRY THIS

Explore your relationship with food.

1. Begin by encouraging yourself to make healthy food choices. Plan what you want to eat and go to the grocery store with a list, being sure not to leave home on an empty stomach so you won't be tempted into impulse buying.

2. When you're at home, try eating a meal without engaging in any other activity, including talking. Eat slowly, placing your full attention on what you're eating and drinking. Experience every taste, pausing to notice any sensations of feeling full.

3. Over time, make connections to the consequences of your food choices. How do you feel after eating a meal that's sweet, salty, spicy, starchy, or greasy, or one loaded with carbohydrates or dense in protein? Do you feel stuffed or light, sluggish or energized, hyper or dulled? Do you experience anxiety from too much caffeine or a crash after a sugar rush? Do you have a hard time going to sleep or staying asleep due to what you've eaten or drunk? Notice whether bringing mindfulness to eating decreases your cravings and increases your contentment and sense of well-being.

7. Read the Inscription

Mindfulness of the body is recognized as one of the simplest ways of residing in the present moment, fending off the incessant habit of evaluation and recrimination. Emotions and thoughts can be subtle, elusive, turbulent, or flighty, but the body provides trustworthy, direct experience available in the present moment.

Your body is a teaching manual of what you carry in your mind and heart. The pages filled with "shoulds" and "shouldn'ts" are transcribed in your muscles, joints, and organs. Here to be read, your body is inscribed in the language of aches and pains, tension and tightness, numbness and tingles. You only need to learn from your body and read what it's saying.

The body reveals psychological unease—for example, an inability to sit still may point to a restless mind. A heart that feels heavy may indicate sadness. A throbbing head may signal anxiety. By the same token, the body offers ways to calm the mind. If you bring your attention to points of your body where messages of unworthiness or "dis-ease" are held, the mere act of acknowledgment gives space for tension and unpleasant sensations to soften and dissipate.

TRY THIS

For the following five-minute exercise, lie down on your back and relax. Sink into the feeling of your body and the gentle rhythm of your breath. Invite your breath to slow and deepen into abdominal breathing.

1. Bring your attention to sensations in your face, head, and neck; noticing points of tension or tightness, heaviness or pressure. On the out-breath, the "letting go" breath, invite sensations in this area of your body to release, relax, or simply be.

2. Direct your awareness to sensations in your torso, arms, and hands; sensing any areas of tingling or numbness, cold or heat, strain or knots. On the exhalation, encourage sensations in this area of your body to soften, loosen, or be as they are.

3. Notice sensations in your thighs, calves, feet, and toes; feeling for tightness or hardness, soreness or numbness. On the "letting go" breath, allow sensations in this area of your body to release, ease, or just be.

4. End with a full-body cleansing breath. Inhale deeply as you "sweep" your body for any remaining tension from the bottom of your feet, up your spine, to your head. On a long, full exhale, release all "dust and debris" from an imaginary blowhole on top of your head.

8. Explore Sensations Within

When you bring your attention to your body and your sensory experience, you learn how to "work with" both physical and emotional "dis-ease." "Being with" your body as it is and understanding how to work with pain and discomfort establishes a deep intimacy.

In meditation, mindfulness of the body uses body sensation as the "object of attention." Once you're grounded in the physical sensations of breathing, when you notice body sensations you explore them in minute detail: What does each sensation feel like? Is it dense or fluid, warm or cold, tight or relaxed, piercing or soothing, tingling or throbbing? Without analyzing or evaluating whether it feels good or bad or whether you like it or don't like it, you get to know the sensation by delving into it. By not trying to change or resist how you feel, you're more able to "be with" your sensations as they are.

The body scan is a practice used in Jon Kabat-Zinn's MBSR program (Kabat-Zinn 1990, 76–79). In this meditation, you identify sensations by systematically moving your attention from one part of your body to the next, beginning with your toes and feet and ending with your head and scalp. Scanning your body is like being a scientist looking for tiny microbes with a magnifying glass. As in mindfulness of the body meditation, this focused attention enhances concentration and cultivates such qualities as patience, nonstriving, nonjudgment, and letting be.

A full body scan typically takes twenty to forty minutes. But it's not necessary to follow any set pattern or length of time. In two to three full sweeps, you can scan your body for tension from the tips of your toes to the crown of your head by zeroing in on segments, such as lower extremities, torso, and face/head. While it's most common to scan from the bottom up, for some purposes it can be helpful to reverse direction.

Both mindfulness of the body meditation and the body scan teach you to steer toward discomfort by simply acknowledging what's there. You notice how fighting against what you feel only increases the pain and discomfort you wish weren't there. Both practices prepare you for the subsequent meditations of mindfulness of thoughts and mindfulness of emotions (parts 2 and 3). Through "working with" your body, you're preparing for the work of counterintuitively steering toward disturbing thoughts and distressing emotions.

TRY THIS

An audio version of this meditation is available for download at www.newharbinger.com/27954.

Carve out ten minutes (or longer, so you can go more deeply into this meditation on the body). Lie on your back, with your legs slightly apart and stretched in front of you; arms straight but relaxed, away from your sides; and palms loosely opened and turned toward the sky. Gently close your eyes. Allow your jaw to soften, allow your tongue to drop, and allow your eyeballs to sink into their sockets. Feel how the weight of your body is held by the earth. Notice the current of your breath in your body as you sink and dissolve into the present moment.

Once your mind is settled, when you clearly notice a body sensation, gently bring your focused attention to the sensation, with a kind intention to be fully present. Steer toward the sensation. What does it feel like? Is there tightness or tension? Tingling or trembling? Heat or cold? Numbness or itchiness? Obvious or subtle vibrations? Notice sensations both on your skin and deep within your body; feel into your muscles, bones, organs, tendons, blood flow, and pulsations.

Without resisting the sensations, simply acknowledge what you physically feel. You can know resistance when you're judging, clinging to, avoiding, or denying the sensation. Rather than analyzing or evaluating your experience, explore and get to intimately know what your body feels like. Imagine breathing into and out from the sensation, making room for sensations to run their course or simply be. Or just keep breathing and acknowledge what it is you're feeling, because acknowledgment itself can be enough to soothe and soften.

As you make room for sensations to be, notice whether they soften, dissolve, or dissipate. If they remain the same, observe whether acknowledging sensations just as they are enables you to stay with them—to experience them without feeling the need to do anything about them.

When your mind wanders into a stream of thought, return to your "object of attention"—body sensations. When your mind goes into evaluating, assessing, or interpreting a physical sensation, come back to the direct experience of your body. When the physical sensation is no longer central or if it's too painful or difficult to stay with, return to the sensations of breathing.

End this meditation by returning to your breath, floating upon a few breath currents. Do you feel greater intimacy with your body?

9. Hold Court

When you take your seat to meditate, you ground yourself in the present moment and establish your presence. You summon your body to take you into moment-to-moment awareness and be open and receptive to what's here. You call upon your body to sit erect, balanced, and relaxed but alert so it can usher your mind to be steady, even, awake, and calm.

Your posture embodies your attitude. When you sit still and steady on your meditation pillow or chair, you take hold of a sense of nobility or grace. You stand tall and stable as the giant sequoia or lie balanced and serene like the floating lotus. You're then ready and equipped to "meet and greet" yourself in the present moment.

Establishing presence in meditation invites taking this same embodied presence with you through your day. You learn to weather howling winds as does the majestic sequoia or stay afloat on turbulent water as does the sacred lotus. You're ready to meet whatever comes your way, welcomed or not.

In Maurice Sendak's (1963) classic picture book *Where the Wild Things Are*, the hero, Max, demonstrates how the right way is typically seen as the wrong way. In a decision that appeared crazy and impulsive, he took a journey across the rough and ominous sea, to where the wild things lived. He went *toward* what was threatening and scary. In that trek to confront his fears, he found strength, courage, and perseverance, and he discovered himself along the way. With his robe, his crown, his lance, and the way he commanded attention, Max radiated presence. He didn't just talk the talk, he walked the walk. Max exuded royalty in the noble qualities he cultivated. When he met the wild things, Max looked at them as they "roared their terrible roar." He stood tall, one hand holding firm to the lance he planted in the ground, the other palm out and fingers up, signaling "Stop!" Max yelled, "BE STILL!" and the wild things froze in their tracks. Max tamed his demons!

When you ground yourself in your body in meditation and hold a posture of nobility, you can "show up" with the confidence to make peace with *your* fears. You can let go of the rules and regulations that keep you hiding under the covers and instead open to whatever you find in plain view or lurking in some dark corner. When you take your seat on that meditation pillow or chair, that rock, or that patch of sand, you're putting on robes sewn with threads of strength, humility, and compassion: qualities for your journey into the land of "embodied" self-esteem. Whether you're stopping to meditate or just going about your day, you can "hold court" in your body when your attention wanders, when your mind is restless, or when your emotions become unruly.

TRY THIS

Take your seat to meditate, either on a chair or on a pillow. If sitting in a chair, place your feet flat on the floor. If sitting on a meditation pillow, or *zafu*, cross your legs evenly and position your buttocks on the edge of the pillow. This keeps your back from swaying, elongates your spine, and lets your knees rest on the floor. If you don't have a meditation pillow, use a pillow that is several inches thick or a blanket that is repeatedly folded to achieve a height that's comfortable for you. Gently close your eyes. Feel how your body is sitting, and feel your contact with the floor and chair or pillow.

Mindfully move your body as you settle into the posture. Allow your shoulders to fall and relax. Square your head, moving your chin slightly toward your chest. Place your hands on your thighs, with palms up or down. Sit upright and balanced, not leaning forward or backward or tilted to one side. With an erect spine, feel how the lower half of your body is rooted to the earth as the upper half reaches toward the sky. Do you feel the length and depth of this posture? If your palms are faced up, do you feel the gentle effect of your chest lifting and your heart opening, creating an attitude of receptivity? If your palms are faced down, do you feel the subtle effect of heaviness and solidness, creating the effect of being grounded? Slightly raise the corners of your mouth into a half smile, or "Buddha smile": the same quiet, calm, confident smile that is seen on Buddha's face in many representations of him, which reminds us to rest in the present moment with awareness and compassion and to let go of our need to strive, compare, judge, and intellectualize. Sense how this very subtle movement has a big effect in lifting your heart and lightening your spirit. Feel into the framework of your body—sitting tall, solid, and stable with relaxed alertness. Note how you feel emotionally and physically.

10. Integrate and Harmonize

Sometimes you may feel so edgy that you can't still your mind to meditate. Mindful movement practices are blessings for settling the mind and easing mental and emotional turmoil. Whether you're walking down the street or drinking a cup of tea, your body is in almost constant motion. The more you enter into awareness of your body in all your actions throughout the day, the deeper your connection to the present moment and the greater your capacity to be truly yourself. We'll focus first on yoga, then on qigong (step 11) and walking meditation (step 12), but you can use any practice that focuses on the breath, movement, and awareness. You can also incorporate mindfulness into any daily activity, such as washing dishes, to calm and ground yourself.

Yoga, meaning "to integrate" in Sanskrit, reestablishes the union and balance of mind and body. Through postures, yoga corrects learned patterns stored in the "memory of the body" and the "muscles of the mind." There are upside-down, twisted, contorted, stretching, and balancing postures. As you learn how to move into and out of these challenging positions, you gain insight on how you get into and out of entanglements of the mind.

Yoga calls upon a curious, flexible mind and a willing, elastic body to stay in harmony and balance while being constantly challenged to stay relaxed and alert. It also supports a sense of composure in challenging situations, such as times you're not feeling as competent as others—yoga students or otherwise!

Yoga teaches valuable lessons, such as how to "work with" striving. You notice how trying too hard tightens your muscles, while relaxing loosens them so you can stretch and twist without exertion. This helps you stop chasing after goals motivated by "musts" and "shoulds" and loosens the hold of mental preoccupations and emotional fluctuations. As you discover ways to work with physical discomfort, you begin to grasp how to work with emotional weaknesses, limitations, and vulnerabilities. The strength, mobility, and balance that yoga teaches vividly demonstrate the potent influence of the breath on physical and emotional pain. You learn how to conserve rather than waste energy and how to use your breath to release tension in your mind and tightness in your body. When you hold your breath, your ability to do the poses is greatly hampered, but when you breathe loudly, deeply, and fully, there is greater flow in movement. You can apply the lessons learned in yoga, like all mindfulness practices, to the art of living.

As you come to know your body on a deeply intimate level, you come to recognize when you're pulled and pushed into holding on to what feels good and avoiding what feels bad. Like all mindfulness practices, yoga is about finding ways to *let go*, such as further releasing into the stretch with the out-breath or discerning straining from stretching so you know to stop striving. Yoga teaches you how to become alert to early warning signs of emotional tension and how to work within the limits of your comfort zone without judging how you're doing. You discover that place of balance where you're neither overdoing nor under-doing it. As you find this "middle path," you practice being where you are, as opposed to trying to be somewhere else or something else. You learn to make the life practice of yoga your own and live from a place of union and balance of mind and body.

Try This

Begin this mini yoga exercise standing, with enough room on either side to spread your arms wide.

Mountain pose. Stand tall, with your feet a few inches apart. Bend your knees a little, and tuck your buttocks in slightly. This places your lower back in a neutral position and lengthens your spine. Balance your head between your shoulders, with your chin parallel to the floor. Rest your arms to each side, with your palms open. Allow your shoulders to fall and relax. Invite your breath to slow and deepen.

Swan dive. On your next full inhalation, spread your arms wide, like a bird spreading its wings, with your palms facing up, slowly reaching toward the sky. As your palms meet at their highest point (above your head), exhale and turn your palms outward, slowly lowering your arms and reaching toward the floor as you bend forward at your waist with a flat back, as if you were diving like a swan, but without straining.

Rag doll. From swan dive, relax into a stretch so that your head and arms dangle loosely as you bend at the waist. As you hang like a rag doll, notice what happens to any physical and emotional tightness when your breath is rapid and shallow versus long and deep. Notice how your breath affects your ability to sustain the posture and stretch farther. Bring your attention to the out-breath—the letting-go breath—and sense whether stretching increases when you breathe out. Imagine breathing "into" any regions of tightness or tension, further loosening the stretch. Invite yourself to relax and sink into this stretch while you continue to breathe deeply from your belly, taking the opportunity to practice nonstriving, nonjudgment, and patience.

Be aware of judgmental thoughts, such as *I'm so out of shape, I can't touch the floor.* When your attention wanders, reel your mind back to this stretch. Take the "middle path" by neither overdoing nor underdoing it. Know that if your body feels strained from holding the pose too long, you can slowly come out of the posture and rest in mountain pose at any time.

Mountain pose (again). After several breaths in rag doll, on your next inhalation, slowly uncurl from the bottom up, one vertebra at a time, your head being last to uncurl, until you're standing once again in mountain pose. Breathing fully and deeply, bring your awareness to the sensation of your body as a whole. Do you now have a greater sense of an integrated mind and body?

11. Flow with Energy

Similar to yoga, qigong is another mindful movement practice. Qigong literally means "the cultivation of energy or life force." Qigong recognizes the universe as made of energy and focuses on this energy, both inside and outside the body. As your practice of qigong deepens, your sense of your body shifts from the feeling that your body is solid to the feeling that it's a stream of energy or sensations. This loosens the hold of a fixed sense of self—a certain state you may be looking to hold on to that's locked in place and time. In qigong, you tap into the infinite source of energy and feel a sense of spaciousness and "self in process." Moving with a sense of fullness rather than scarcity invites feelings of unworthiness to disperse and feelings of wholeness to awaken.

Cultivating energy through qigong begins to tip over the hurdle between you and others. Your sense of self is not limited to the size of your head or the shape of your body, but is open and expansive because energy is boundless and abundant. While you make purposeful effort, you simultaneously surrender. You are "one" with "the source."

TRY THIS

The following qigong movement is taught by mindfulness teacher Bob Stahl in his MBSR class.

Stand tall and balanced in mountain pose (see step 10). Place your arms to each side, with your palms loosely curved and your shoulders down and relaxed. Feel into the framework of this posture—feel into your body—and the rhythmic flow of your breath. Expand your awareness to the field of energy or vibrations inside your body and in the surrounding space. Surrender to the present moment.

Breathing in—energy rising. With a long, deep inhalation, slowly raise your arms in front of you, with elbows, wrists, palms, and fingers loosely curved, until your hands are chest high, as you sense or imagine energy rising from your palms.

Breathing in again—energy expanding. With a further inhalation and your knees still bent, slowly spread your arms wide like a bird, with elbows, wrists, palms, and fingers loosely curved, until your arms are fully out to your sides, as you feel or envision energy expanding from your palms.

Breathing out—energy collecting. On the exhalation, straighten your knees and gently and slowly lower your arms, with elbows, wrists, palms, and fingers loosely curved, as you sense or "tune into" energy flowing into your body from your palms.

Repeat this three-part movement several times, slowly and rhythmically. Remember to inhale deeply and then further inhale before you exhale; bend your knees during the inhalations and straighten them for the exhalation; and keep your elbows, wrists, hands, and palms softly bent and curved during all movements.

When you're ready, come to your final movement and stand in mountain pose with your eyes closed. Open your awareness to the feeling of your body as a whole and the energy within and outside your body.

12. Greet the Earth

The body is the vehicle of the mind. If you think that you're not as good as others, you may slouch, avoid meeting people's gazes, or stare into space. If you think that, alternatively, you're better than others, you may walk with your chin up, looking down your nose at people, not really seeing or hardly noticing who's near. If you're impatient, you may rush; if you're agitated, you may pace; if you're scared, you may run; if you're tired, you may stop (Kabat-Zinn 1990, 114). When you're lost in thought, you may arrive at a destination without ever experiencing the journey.

In walking meditation, you mindfully walk back and forth for ten to twenty paces in each direction, slowly and deliberately, bringing your attention to sensations in your feet and legs or to your whole body moving, either with simultaneous awareness of your breath or coordinating your breath with your steps. You gaze softly down at the ground immediately in front of you, watching not the motion of your feet, but the workings of your mind.

Walking meditation can also entail walking slowly with your gaze open to what's nearest you, occasionally stopping to inhale any scents, feel the air on your skin, and notice intricacies of hues, texture, and tone in the objects around you. There's no right way to do walking meditation. In his book *Peace Is Every Step*, Thich Nhat Hanh suggests: "If you feel happy, peaceful, and joyful while you are walking, you are practicing correctly. Be aware of the contact between your feet and the Earth. Walk as if you are kissing the Earth with your feet" (Nhat Hanh 1992, 28). He also encourages smiling.

The purpose of walking meditation is to not try to get anywhere except into the present moment—to walk not for the purpose of arriving at a destination but for the purpose of being fully present in every step. Walking meditation teaches you how to experience life as a process, not a goal—this is a central aspect of mindful self-esteem.

The unfamiliar stillness experienced in walking meditation can bring some people discomfort. It can also be hard to go slowly, for fear of not accomplishing daily responsibilities. Or you may be used to striving to be somewhere other than where you are (that is, keeping busy), as a way to avoid the uninvited concerns of weak self-esteem and unfinished emotional business. But this short-term solution leads to long-term issues. Walking meditation brings you into balance with any extreme—from tiredness or agitation to calmness and composure—so you can dust worry off your feet and enjoy the walk.

When you feel the ground with your feet, feel the movement of your body, and feel the beauty of the path, you feel connected to the earth. This arouses a sense of gratitude for your body because your body takes you where you want to go. As you grasp the complexity of the seemingly simple act of walking—which requires balance, coordination, energy, and ability—you begin to understand the meaning of Thich Nhat Hanh's statement "The miracle is to walk on earth" (1976, 11).

If you're like most people, as you travel through your day you sometimes notice that you're not really watching where you're going. Other times, you're moving too quickly or mindlessly to notice and appreciate your surroundings. As an awareness practice, walking meditation is considered a gateway for mindfulness in daily life, bringing you more in touch with yourself on your journey.

TRY THIS

Find a quiet room or a place outside where you can walk for ten to twenty paces in one direction. Stand in mountain pose (see step 10) at one end of your chosen space.

1. With mindful attention, shift your weight to one foot as the other foot rises from the ground ever so slowly. Feel the sensations, both big and small, in your body as you do so. Notice what makes the lifting occur. Is there a feeling of pulling? Is there a sense of heaviness or one of lightness? As you exaggerate the movement of walking, observe whether your mind wants to either cling to or avoid this experience, saying *I like this* or *I don't like this.*

2. Glide your lifted foot forward, feeling into sensations in your body. Is the motion smooth, or is it jerky? If you're feeling impatient, agitated, calm, or settled, do you move more quickly or more slowly? What happens to your balance when your mind is attentive versus distracted? Notice when judgment occurs. How much do you identify with how you're doing?

3. Plant the heel of your forward foot on the ground, then your toes, noticing your balance and weight distribution, the angle of your body, and sensations throughout your body. With the sense of solidity when planting your foot on the ground, is there also a sense of impermanence—the arising and passing of all things—as you attend to the process? With all these actions coming together, notice a sense of nothing to hold on to.

4. Seamlessly begin to shift your weight to the other foot as you slowly raise—glide—plant the other foot on the ground, walking forward step by step into each moment.

5. When you reach the end of your walking space, ever so minutely, with your full awareness, make a slow turn in the opposite direction as you continue to walk step by step, moment by moment. Focus not on different aspects of walking, but on one aspect at a time, keeping your gaze right in front of

you. This strengthens your concentration. While your primary focus of attention is on walking, maintain awareness of breathing on the side. As with all other mindfulness meditations, when your mind wanders, reel it back to the object of your attention—in this case, the sensation of walking.

6. Walk with awareness back and forth in your space, with keen attention and with intention to not get anywhere except into the present moment. As you're practicing, be present with the sensations of walking, meeting yourself on the path of the present moment, saying *Hello* to the workings of your mind. On your final turn, stand in mountain pose. Bask in stillness.

13. The Lesson of Seaweed

Through these "foundational practices," you've experienced being—in both stillness and movement—without resistance, staying grounded and open to whatever comes your way. You've set the conditions for a self-esteem that's a relationship with life.

TRY THIS

The following qigong move is also taught by Bob Stahl in his MBSR class. Imagine that you're a giant frond of seaweed in a kelp forest on a splendid summer day. Your feet are rooted to the ocean floor, and your head is touching the water's surface as your top leaf moves with the gentle waves. Your arms are slowly swinging as your long limbs filled with leaves sway or dance light-heartedly. Every inch of your stalk torso is strong and sturdy, yet smooth and pliable. Silver streams of sunlight penetrate the water, infusing your seaweed body with warmth and sustenance.

In time comes a change of weather, turning the calm water turbulent. Above, the wind blows and rain falls. But regardless of the conditions, your seaweed body stays supple and flexible, moving back and forth, side to side, stretching and curving far and wide, mindfully attuned to the ocean currents without resistance. Your seaweed base stays grounded, deeply rooted to the ocean floor, and your torso remains anchored with the breath of the waves, gently rising and falling. One with others in the kelp forest in the aqueous flow of life, you reside in dynamic movement. In time, the weather system moves on and the storm waves begin to settle. The movement of your seaweed body begins to decrease. The ocean slowly returns to calm. You stand tall, flexible, and motionless in the stillness of the ocean, abiding in "mindful seaweed self-esteem."

Part 2

Thinking and the Mind

The intention in this part of the book is to cultivate qualities for unconditional self-acceptance through thinking practices based on the wisdom of paradox. Through the essential paradox of turning toward that which you resist, acceptance teaches you how to "be with" what is, just the way it is, not the way you wish it were. Acceptance requires cultivating other "pillars of mindfulness": nonjudging, beginner's mind, nonstriving, letting be, patience, and trust as self-reliance. Rather than trying to analyze and explain how to get from one place or state of affairs to another, you learn to pay attention to the present moment and be the person you already are. This ignites a change from a self-esteem driven by "doing"—striving to be someone you're not—to a self-esteem cultivated by "being"—witnessing your own unfolding nature.

14. An Impartial Witness

It's all too common to move through the day with an overlay of judgment: a constant critique in which you judge whether you like or don't like what's happening; decide whether you're good or bad; and evaluate whether you've succeeded or failed. Mindfulness teacher Gil Fronsdal likens experiencing life with this overlay of judgment to driving a car with a film of dirt on the windshield day after day (Fronsdal 2008). You're so used to having to peer through the haze, you don't even notice it's there. But you can realize that thoughts that contain words like "should," "shouldn't," "must," and "mustn't" point to underlying judgments about what's good or bad and what's right or wrong.

Judgment often fuels negative emotions, such as anger, frustration, and disappointment. Judgmental thoughts can really take you on a loop because they create a cyclone of story lines such as *I'm such an idiot. I'll never get anywhere.* Adding to the damage, the stories aren't even true. Still, you get down on yourself for thinking that you should be someone you're not or doing something you're not. Even when you judge yourself positively, this can be a problem too: sooner or later, disappointment sets in because what you've evaluated as good or successful doesn't seem to last very long or measure up to expectations.

Removing your overlay of judgment is like washing the film from your windshield. The world looks clear. You become an impartial witness, allowing things to be as they actually exist. Your thoughts are just thoughts, not definitions.

Nonjudging

Nonjudging means bringing an attitude of neutral observation to any encounter, without labeling things as good or bad or resisting the encounter. Contrary to your natural human tendency to judge your experiences, mindfulness teaches you to simply observe your experiences, because this is what leads to insight. Nonjudging doesn't mean eradicating judgmental thoughts. It means that if judgmental thoughts arise, you notice them without acting on them. Instead of using a judgmental thought as a jumping-off point for other thoughts, you simply think, *There's a judgmental thought.*

TRY THIS

How do you begin to cultivate the quality of nonjudging? Start by recognizing when your windshield needs washing!

Notice if you're thinking in value judgments such as good and bad, right and wrong, should and shouldn't, or fair and unfair. If you're saying to yourself something like *I'm stupid and worthless because I just can't get it*, recognize this as judgment leading you into false interpretations and seducing you into identifying with them. If you're feeling the resulting emotions of hopelessness or worthlessness, identify this as the emotional fallout of judgment. The following specific exercise is adapted from Christopher Germer (2009, 113).

For one hour today, bring your awareness to how often you look at the world through the hazy windshield of judgment. Every time you notice a judgmental thought, tally it—put a penny in a pouch, or put a bead in a cup. You can use whatever small objects and whatever container you have handy. At the end of one hour, count how many pennies, beads, or other objects you've accumulated. Do you have five? A hundred? The number doesn't say anything about you—it simply signifies how much you may practice not acting on judgmental thoughts. If you have a thought that the number is good or bad, put another penny in the pouch!

15. Stop the Sorting

Nonjudging implies that there's no such thing as success or failure, right or wrong, or winning or losing. Mistakes simply happen. "A paradox in mindulness practice is that we never get it right, and we never get it wrong" (Germer, Siegel, and Fulton 2005, 114). 7Your worth isn't measured by the result or outcome of your efforts. What really matters is the journey: how you come face-to-face with your experience. When you view life's difficulties as challenges rather than obstacles, they become opportunities for growth. "Working with" difficult situations can unlock new knowledge and provide the energy to set you free.

There's tremendous freedom when you remove judgment from your life. Rather than seeing yourself as a victim of circumstance, you see options and possibilities. In the words of Byron Katie, teacher of a method of self-inquiry and author of the book *Loving What Is*, "Everything happens *for* you not *to* you" (Katie 2002, 227).

TRY THIS

Formal and informal mindfulness exercises share the common features of *stop*, *observe*, and *return*. Stop refers to disengaging from how you're automatically reacting; *observe* refers to bringing your attention to your thoughts, emotions, and physical sensations; and *return* refers to bringing your awareness back to what's occurring in the present moment (Germer, Siegel, and Fulton 2005, 227).

MBSR has an informal practice called STOP, an acronym for Stop, Take a breath, Observe, Proceed. You stop what you're doing, take a breath several times mindfully; observe your thoughts, emotions, and body sensations, acknowledging and inviting the release of obsessive thinking, reactive emotions, and physical tension; and proceed from this state of mindful awareness (Stahl and Goldstein 2010, 60–61). The following informal practice uses the components of stop, return, and observe to specifically cultivate nonjudgment.

When you notice a judgmental thought, stop for just a few minutes to take *1-2-3 Action*:

1. *Thoughts.* Acknowledge your judgmental thought. Step back to observe it briefly.

2. *Emotions.* Notice the impact of your judgmental thought on your emotions. With neutral attention, briefly notice what feelings are present.

3. *Body.* Work with your body through breathing. Use mindful breathing to create a pause and unhook from the judgmental thought. Take a few deep, long abdominal breaths to engage your

relaxation response. Bring your attention to places of stored tension and tightness in your body. Imagine breathing into and out of places of stored tension. Alternatively, infuse each in-breath and out-breath with the healing aspirations described in step 5. For example, on the in-breath, say, *Nonjudgment*; on the out-breath, say, *Challenge*, *Opportunity*, or *Growth*.

Action. Influence your actions. From this nonjudgmental state, invite actions that encourage feelings of positivity—for example, walking, reaching out to a friend, or engaging in mindful movement.

Write a journal entry that describes your experience. How did you feel before taking *1-2-3 Action*? How do you feel now?

16. Don't Know

If you don't have an attitude of curiosity, the freedom to explore and know yourself as an ever-changing flow of experience may play second fiddle to the need to hold tightly to a fixed sense of self. In an attempt to seek security in an uncertain world, you may strive to fill in the blanks with answers that aren't necessarily true or correct. Often these answers are based on your past impressions, your conclusions, or your judgments about similar previous experiences. In your need to find a solid base, you may put so much effort into looking for answers that you forget to ask the questions themselves.

Mindfulness focuses on gaining insight by asking two fundamental questions: What leads to suffering, and what leads to the end of suffering? These questions are followed by two more questions: What are you doing that's skillful, and what are you doing that's unskillful? Focusing on these questions leads to a spirit of curiosity and active engagement in life.

Beginner's Mind

Mindfulness cultivates beginner's mind: looking at things as if for the first time, without assumptions. When you employ beginner's mind, you meet life with an attitude of curiosity; every moment is a new beginning. This gets you out of the judgmental "good versus bad," "this versus that" thinking that automatically puts you somewhere other than where you are. All sorts of possibilities are created, because you're paying attention to everything occurring in the present moment and being okay in the confusion, in the not knowing. In the words of Lao-tzu, paradoxically, "The more you know, the less you understand" (1988, Epigram 47).

Often used to demonstrate beginner's mind, otherwise known as "don't know mind," is the well-known story of the empty teacup. A professor visited a famous Zen master to converse about Zen. While the professor was talking, the Zen master quietly began to serve them both tea. He filled the professor's cup to the brim, then continued to pour. Thinking this incredible, the professor shouted: "Stop! The cup is already full! No more will go in!" In response, the Zen master declared, "I can't show you Zen unless you first empty your cup."

In our need to know and to compete with one another to prove our worth, we fill our minds with defensive clutter—judgments, assumptions, interpretations, foregone conclusions, and erroneous beliefs. But when you allow for not knowing, the world opens up. You can truly be present to your experiences, including during the pouring of tea.

Try This

Begin to cultivate beginner's mind as a way of being by noticing your assumptions.

- Observe when you make assumptions in common, ordinary occurrences. An example is when you're driving behind a car that's going fifteen miles per hour under the speed limit and you think, *He's probably distracted by talking on the cell phone* or *She's probably too old to be driving.*

- When faced with challenging situations, such as an interpersonal conflict or an event in which you'll be judged, notice whether you're predicting the outcome—whether fearing the worst, or self-assuredly projecting the best.

- When presented with challenging tasks that stretch your capabilities, notice whether you're tensing up from not knowing what to do—in other words, assuming that you don't have what it takes.

Every time you react on autopilot by making assumptions, neglecting to explore creative solutions, or feeling bored, frustrated, or insecure as a result of judgmental, assuming thoughts, practice beginner's mind and see what happens!

17. See the Whole Elephant

Our concept of reality is often based on only a limited version of what's actually present. We get pieces of experiences and construct a story, living life according to a script. We know the world through stories with fixed beginnings and endings, and because they fit together in a sort of scheme, we believe that we have all the necessary pieces to complete the puzzle of who we are. However, these pictures are often not very pretty, and they lead to our believing that the unworthiness we feel is the result of our not being good enough in some way.

But if you can relax your mind and open to possibilities with beginner's mind, there's no end to the awe and wonder as truths unfold in time. "In the beginner's mind there are many possibilities, but in the expert's there are few" (Roshi 1986, 21).

"The Blind Men and the Elephant" is an Indian fable often used to demonstrate beginner's mind. A sweet version of this story is the picture book *Seven Blind Mice* by Ed Young (2002), in which seven different colored blind mice find a mysterious thing (an elephant) by the pond. One by one they go out to explore what it could possibly be, and based on the part of the elephant they touch, each returns with a different idea. For example, the mouse who touches the elephant's tail thinks it's a snake; the mouse who feels the elephant's tusk thinks it's a spear; and the mouse who rubs the elephant's ear thinks it's a fan. When the seventh mouse investigates the whole mysterious thing, its true nature becomes clear. In a way, each of the other six mice was right. But because they had not "seen" the whole elephant, they were also wrong. Paradoxically, the less they knew, the more they thought they knew.

TRY THIS

Think of a story you tell about yourself or have been led to believe, perhaps one that has caused you to view yourself negatively and created a burden of guilt, shame, or resentment. For example, if your parents divorced, perhaps you grew up believing it was your fault because you weren't good enough. Consider that your story is based on limited and false assumptions, and explore the possibility that there may be more to it than "meets the eye." Perhaps there were external forces beyond your understanding at work. For example, perhaps your mother divorced your father because she felt betrayed by his secret affair. Write your preconceived story in your journal, noting assumptions and conclusions that are based on emotional reasoning, not facts. Then ask yourself: *How would I be different if it were not for this belief? How would I feel? What might I do?*

18. Eat As If It's the First Time

Beginner's mind enables you to experience life to its fullest, not in a way that's limited by your expectations. To introduce the concept of beginner's mind, MBSR uses an exercise in which participants each eat a single raisin. They're asked to explore the raisin in slow motion, one sense at a time—sight, smell, touch, sound, and taste—as though it were something completely new to them. Without interpreting what they notice or what it reminds them of, they simply identify its qualities, such as its color, texture, and fragrance. This exercise demonstrates how bringing awareness to any activity, even those that we take most for granted, fosters a deep appreciation of what each moment holds (Kabat-Zinn 1990, 27–28).

Eating a raisin with beginner's mind often stands in sharp contrast to the more typical experience of gobbling a handful of raisins all at once and barely tasting them or even noticing they've been eaten. When you eat a raisin with beginner's mind, you experience it with deep awareness. Sometimes you can get a sensation of satisfaction or even a subtle sense of fullness just by eating a single raisin! When you reside in deep awareness, you fully inhabit yourself and all of life.

TRY THIS

A common way to cultivate mindfulness in daily life is by eating in slow motion. Begin by sitting down to eat a meal alone, without distractions. Resolve to focus only on eating—don't incorporate another activity into your meal, such as reading, working on the laptop, talking on the phone, or listening to music.

1. Look at the food on your plate. Notice all the shapes, colors, and textures. Think about how you would describe the way your food looks to someone who had never seen it before. Do the same for your drink.

2. Pay attention to the different aromas and fragrances of your food and drink. Do you pick up the scents by inhaling closely, or do the essences permeate the room?

3. Slowly begin to eat, continuing to engage your senses. As you eat, do you hear crunching, popping, or sizzling? When you drink, do you hear slurping, bubbling, or sipping?

4. Savor each bite of food. Be totally present with what you're eating. Is it sweet, sour, salty, or pungent? Notice how the taste of the food changes as you chew it, and notice the sensations of chewing and swallowing.

5. Be aware of your actions as you eat. Notice how you bring the fork or spoon to your mouth and place it down again, how you cut the food, and how you mix the items on the plate or keep them separate.

6. Observe how you feel as you eat. Do you sense pleasure? Gratification? Gratitude? Disappointment? Surprise? Comfort?

7. Notice if it's difficult to experience the food just as it is, without measuring it against expectations. Do you find yourself evaluating the meal every few minutes, or even with every bite? If so, reel your mind back to eating. Stay with your senses of sight, taste, touch, sound, and smell as your "objects of attention." Treat this exercise as a meditation on eating.

What was it like to bring beginner's mind to a meal you may have had a hundred times before, with every taste a brand-new experience? Can you imagine approaching everything you do with beginner's mind? What would that be like?

19. Being vs. Doing

Your search for external validation to prove your worth to yourself has been guided by judgment, accompanied by mistaken assumptions, and fueled by striving—an incessant drive to push forward, compete, and aim for results that focus on the future. But the road to *more* only leads to greater feelings of inadequacy and worthlessness, because there's never enough. The farther along this road you are, the farther you are from imagining what life would be like without striving, and the more distant you become from knowing your inner worth.

According to Bronnie Ware, palliative nurse and author of *The Top Five Regrets of the Dying*, the most common regret at the end of life is "I wish I'd had the courage to live a life true to myself, not the life others expected of me" (Ware 2012, 34). The second most common regret is "I wish I didn't work so hard" (66).

Nonstriving

Nonstriving is defined as not trying to get anywhere except into the present moment. Nonstriving means replacing the myth that life is happening somewhere else with the belief that what's happening now is what really matters. Nonstriving places attention on being, not doing; on seeing, not seeking. It's process oriented, not goal oriented. Instead of chasing after goals motivated by "musts" and "shoulds" and thinking *If only things were different*, you simply open to the present moment just as it is, just as you are. As Lao-tzu said, paradoxically, "The way to do is to be" (1944, 9). On the path of mindfulness, true self-esteem is being true to yourself.

TRY THIS

As you move about your day, notice when you're striving. Striving might feel like overthinking the problem, over-looking the obvious answer, or overfocusing on the result. You may be aware of an undercurrent of anxiety, fear, or worry fueling the drive. Perhaps there's a sense of pulling against or pushing forward—either running away by trying to compensate for past failings or rushing toward by attempting to accomplish goals.

When you sense yourself striving, send out an *SOS*:

S: Send a signal. Alert yourself to slow down. Breathe deeply.

O: Orient. Get your bearings on how you're striving.

How are your thoughts contributing to overthink-ing, overlooking, or overfocusing? For example, you may be thinking that you can't find the solution to a problem or won't have the time or resources necessary to complete a task. How are your emotions fueling the thought? For example, you may regret that you didn't learn the skill, you may obsess and ruminate on the task, and you may disregard such basic needs as eating well or exercising.

S: Soften. Bring in aid by releasing tension in your body through movement, in one of the following ways.

- Yoga: Twist your body to the right and the left, hang like a rag doll, raise and lower your arms wide like a bird, roll your head, lift your shoulders and let them fall, or use any position or movement that "works with" tension.

- Qigong: Use qigong and move like a giant frond of seaweed in turbulent water; raise, collect, and expand energy with the movement of your arms and hands; or use any movement with your hands to feel energy.

- Walking meditation: Walk back and forth slowly and deliberately, or walk quietly outside, not trying to get anywhere except into the present moment.

Be aware of your intentions in practicing SOS. Are you trying to feel better about yourself or trying to force an outcome? *Trying* to practice nonstriving feeds the very striving you want to avoid. Identify your intention as simply to observe striving and work with your *relationship* to it.

20. Release the Grip

Striving has its costs. It's ineffective and inefficient. In your quest for external validation, striving has caused you to exert so much energy that stopping and tuning into what's happening right now probably feels like exactly the wrong thing to do. For many, striving is motivated by being a highly conscientious person and having excessive personal standards. But it's all too easy to overcommit, rush to meet deadlines, put out persistent effort to not let yourself and others down, and then burn out! Even when you do fulfill your goals, you may feel disappointed and depleted because your energy has been directed away from yourself and toward external measures of success.

Striving sets up a vicious cycle. Although your desires may be positive—for example, you may desire to feel good about yourself—the mere thought that you should feel a certain way causes you to strive for it. Ironically, this in and of itself creates increased striving and decreased happiness.

Nonstriving doesn't mean being lazy or uncaring, or not having desires or interests. In fact, it means the opposite. Nonstriving means having clear intentions, staying focused, being a keen observer, and allowing life to unfold as it will.

Nonstriving is like going down rapids in a kayak. You don't fight against the current, but neither do you just sit there and let it toss you about. You also don't fix your gaze on the rock wall you're trying to avoid. Rather, you paddle with deep concentration to stay on course, and you keep your eyes on the river ahead. When you let go of your fears (smashing into the rock wall) and your expectations (staying perfectly on course), you allow the experience to naturally unfold. As you let mindfulness happen, you and the river of life are one and the same.

Evan Weselake's (2004, 156) personal story of surviving an avalanche offers a great lesson on nonstriving. In 2003, Evan was one of thirteen backcountry skiers who were carried down British Columbia's Mount Traviata by a gigantic avalanche and buried under tons of snow. He was unable to move but still able to see some light, and though the snow compressed his chest, he could still somewhat breathe. Initially, Evan reacted with fear and tried to fight against the snow to move, but quickly he lost all breath. Evan was an endurance cyclist and familiar with what's called "bonking"—suddenly feeling unable to go even a tad farther. He had developed the ability to look for inner resources of strength and calm that enabled him to identify wasted energy and redirect it. He recognized the need to "let go." As he relaxed his body, his breathing relaxed, and his need for air lessened. He was rescued several hours later.

TRY THIS

For the following exercise, you'll need a poster-size sheet of paper, a colored piece of chalk or charcoal, and someone who's willing to be your model for a drawing.

Ask your model to strike a pose of any kind and maintain this position for three minutes. With your paper on an easel or table, outline the contours of your model—without looking at the paper, not even for a second. Let go of any notion of what your picture *should* look like. It doesn't matter if the right side of the body doesn't match up with the left side of the body, the eyes are where the nose should be, or there's no room remaining on the paper to include the feet. Rather than the chalk being your tool, let the drawing flow from the chalk. Reside in a spirit of curiosity, fun, and reckless abandonment of the final outcome! When the three minutes have passed, stop wherever you are, and feast your eyes on what you've drawn.

The manner in which you approached this exercise sheds light on how you deal with challenging situations in life. If you found yourself sneaking peeks to produce a better outcome, this may reflect a tendency to struggle to make things happen because you're trying to achieve or prove something. If you felt your efforts to ensure accuracy in your picture decreased your sense of pleasure and increased the feeling of struggling, this may reflect a tendency to get so frustrated or overwhelmed that you make challenging situations more difficult. If you worried that your picture would be awful in some way, this may reflect a tendency to feel like a failure when you're unable to reach your goals.

Through journaling, describe what you learned from this exercise and how you can apply what you learned to your life. If you wish to experiment more as a budding artist and your model is willing to strike a few more poses, see how some more drawings unfold. Invite yourself to *do* less and *be* more. By not trying to force a certain outcome, you become freer.

21. Spin the Wheel of Paradox

Second-century Jewish scholar Simon ben Zoma answers four questions on what makes a person *truly* wise, mighty, rich, or honored (Union for Reform Judaism and URJ Press 2004). The answers are quite different from what we're conditioned to believe, since much of what we think and do comes from a place of striving.

To summarize:

- People who are *wise* are not those who know more but those who learn from everyone. Seeing everyone and everything as a teacher and learning opportunity brings wisdom.

- People who are *mighty* are not those who appear strong but those who conquer their reactive impulses. Listening and compromising requires greater strength and perseverance than forcing one's will on others and the world.

- People who are *rich* are not those who have the most money but those who are content with what they have. Trying to accumulate more and more wealth only leads to greater and greater dissatisfaction. Real wealth comes from appreciating what you have.

- People who are *honored* are not those who are bestowed with titles, recognized with awards, or credited with accomplishments but those who honor others. Striving for outward recognition only leads to further discontent and a weak self-esteem, because true honor lies within.

In other words, there's nothing to chase after. There are no external measures of true success and no need to be separate and distinct to prove your true worth. You can come off the never-ending spiral of wanting more and more and finding less and less. Only when you stop striving and turn your thinking around—on the wheel of paradox—can you truly be the wise, mighty, rich, and honored person you already are!

TRY THIS

The two most prominent kinds of meditation in the Buddhist tradition are *Concentration meditation* and *Insight meditation*. Concentration meditation focuses the mind on a single point—such as a mantra, a phrase, or the breath—to calm, stabilize, and empower the mind. In concentration practices, thoughts, emotions, body sensations, and things you sense (such as sounds) are seen as distractions from the intention of sustaining focus. Insight meditation, or Vipassana, on the other hand, sees thoughts, emotions, body sensations, and other things you sense during meditation as part of the unfolding nature of experience, to be observed and related to with nonjudgmental awareness. This awareness practice leads to insight, which contributes to wisdom. Concentration and Insight meditation complement each other, and Insight meditation has some aspect of concentration embedded in the practice.

In Vipassana meditation, anything you're aware of—your breath, body sensations, sounds, thoughts, and emotions—can be your "object of attention." In MBSR, Jon Kabat-Zinn (1990, 71) teaches meditation by focusing first on the breath, then on touch/body sensation, then on sound, then on thoughts, and finally on "choiceless awareness": opening the field of awareness to all the senses simultaneously.

The following meditation focuses on sound and thoughts as the "objects of attention." Through this meditation, you'll practice the mindfulness directive of "non-doing": "Don't just do something, sit there" (Boorstein, 1996, 3). Begin to enter into the present moment by anchoring yourself to your breath and grounding yourself in your body.

Sound. Open your awareness to your sense of sound. Notice the ever-changing nature of sounds around you—how they come and then go, begin and then end, are loud and then soft, are distant and then near, or are high pitched and then low pitched. Rather than experiencing sounds as an annoyance or a distraction, follow the sounds and note their changing nature.

- When your mind wanders, as it will naturally do, make a mental note *Thinking* and simply reel your mind back to your "object of attention"—sounds.

- Focus on the practice, not the goals of the practice. Drop your expectations. If you feel striving, perhaps in the form of tension, impatience, distraction, or judging, take some moments to simply watch it. Then escort your mind back to your object of attention—sounds.

- Before moving to the next object of attention— thoughts—ground your attention in the sensations of your breath.

Thoughts. Bring your awareness now to your thoughts. Notice your stream of thought flow and ebb, take on a story line, go round and round, feel intense or dull, or take on vivid colors or muted hues. Rather than identifying with your thoughts, observe your thoughts like an impartial witness. Without clinging to them or, alternatively, pushing them away, see your thoughts as "mental formations"—random, nonpersonal events appearing and disappearing. Observe your relationship to your thoughts. Do you notice yourself clinging to thoughts with judgment or striving or, alternatively, avoiding thoughts with impatience or boredom? Can you simply witness your thoughts and let them be? Know that if at any time you feel too uncomfortable, you can anchor yourself in your breath and then return to the object of attention—thoughts.

End this meditation by returning to your breath, riding on the currents of your breath in your body. When you're ready, open your eyes.

22. Let Go of Attachment

The basic premise of Buddhist psychology is that craving—clinging to a particular thought or idea, or clinging to what you want or "need" to have as though you actually have the power to attain it—causes suffering. You get attached to a thought, as if nothing else matters, even when it creates all sorts of problems. The seductive nature of thoughts reels you in because you believe that you *are* the thought, and emotions like fear and anxiety confirm it. Before long, the thought has a hold on you. At the core of issues with self-esteem is how tightly you hold on to thoughts about yourself that perpetuate the belief that you're unworthy, inadequate, or ill-equipped.

But if you apply even a touch of mindfulness and get some distance from the thought, you start noticing you're doing something that's tightening the hold. Perhaps if you viewed the thought differently, it might just lose some of its intensity. You start to see that your angst has less to do with the thought itself and more to do with how you're *relating* to it. What might happen if you just let the thought be? Central to cultivating mindful self-esteem is how you relate to your thoughts. When you change your relationship to your thoughts, you change the way you relate to the experience of being you.

Letting Be

Letting be is defined as accepting things as they are, without grasping onto them or, alternatively, pushing them away. Letting be means letting go of your attachment, not wanting more or less—allowing events to run their course. Your habit of holding on to certain thoughts and ideas may be so engrained that letting them be is no simple matter. But as your mindfulness practice grows, you begin to see the cause-and-effect relationship between clinging and suffering and consider that it might be time to think again! You start to loosen your hold on particular thoughts and let the thoughts go.

When you acknowledge what's present and let it be, you become aware of how you're relating to what arises. You notice your wanting—the inborn tendency to want things to be different. You also notice how this wanting only wants more. As the fruits of mindfulness reveal, nothing is worth grasping onto or identifying with, and you begin to focus on relating to the problem in a non-reactive way.

Letting be is not to be confused with suppressing, repressing, or ignoring your thoughts. "Letting be" and "letting go" are sometimes used interchangeably, because letting be may evolve into letting go. When someone says that you "just need to let go," this may push your striving button, influencing you to try harder to let go. But letting go isn't something to strive for. "Trying" to let go can add yet another level of suffering, because once again you're trying to get somewhere other than where you are!

TRY THIS

Choose a habit of yours. It could be something like drinking coffee, having a glass of wine, surfing the web, or playing video games. Just for today, make an intention to not engage in this behavior. When you feel the energy of this habit—an urge, a strong need, or a temptation to indulge in this behavior—get to know what's wedded to this behavior. Are you pulled toward this behavior because you wish you were doing something else or because you're not looking forward to what you need to do next? Are you feeling irritated or frustrated with the task at hand? Is there some loneliness or feeling of disconnection? Is there a sense of heaviness or constriction that you want to get rid of? Are you feeling tired or experiencing a lack of motivation? Acknowledge what you observe in your mind, emotions, and body, allowing whatever's there to be present, without doing anything or trying to change it. Notice that, paradoxically, when you don't try to impose change, change naturally occurs.

23. Catch a Monkey

Our minds are often so cluttered with thoughts about ourselves that we have endless opportunities to practice letting go. In meditation, you cultivate letting go by allowing each breath, each sensation, each sound, each "object of attention," to be as it is—without clinging to the idea of wishing it to be different. At every turn, you're invited to let go, let go, let go. In fact, shifting from conditional, externally based self-esteem to unconditional, internally experienced self-esteem is primarily about letting go. As you let go of your resistance to the way things are, you relinquish unrealistic expectations that you can never meet and false interpretations that can never bring you ease.

There's a Buddhist psychology lesson on letting go called "How to Catch a Monkey." A small hole is made in a coconut and a banana is placed inside. When a monkey comes along, reaches in, and grasps the banana, it can't pull out its hand. The monkey is easily caught because it never lets go of the banana!

In meditation, you observe how you're relating to your experience. Are you rejecting the experience with impatience, boredom, or sleepiness; or clinging to it with judgment, striving, or mistrust? Can you simply rest in awareness itself?

You may worry that meditation or practicing letting be in everyday life will lead to passivity because you're not striving to get anywhere. But when you let things be, change and movement naturally occur. Letting be pushes the pause button, so you don't get "caught" holding on to ruminations, depressed feelings, or anxious thoughts. You let go of the banana!

TRY THIS

Find a downloadable audio version of this meditation at www.newharbinger.com/27954.

In the following "choiceless awareness" meditation, you open to all the "objects of attention" you've worked with so far—your breath, your body sensations, sounds, and your thoughts—simultaneously. You observe the "object of attention" with "bare attention"—opening your awareness to the sensation without judging, thinking about, or reacting against it.

This is a wonderful meditation to cultivate letting be as you enter into the constant ebb and flow of life's changing nature, finding the balance between intentional effort and letting go into the unfolding of your experiences.

1. Once you've anchored yourself to your breath and grounded yourself in your body and your attention is relaxed and alert, expand your field of awareness

to your breath, body sensations, sounds, and thoughts. Focus on whatever seems to beckon to you. If you keenly feel your breath, float upon its waves. If your body sensations are most vivid, delve deeply into this area. If sounds are what stand out, listen ever so closely. If your thoughts are most noticeable, observe them as "mental formations" coming and going.

2. Shift from sense to sense, allowing your senses to lead you. Consider any sense or sensation not as a distraction, but rather as an open field for curious exploration. Keep your attention on whatever seems most pressing until another sense pulls you in that direction. Ride your current of awareness as it naturally shifts.

3. As with all mindfulness meditations, whenever your mind wanders, bring it back to the "object of attention," in this case whichever sense most captures your attention.

End this meditation by returning to your breath, acknowledging the time you've carved out to "let things be."

24. Stop After the First Arrow

Because we tend to identify with our thoughts and cling to them, when your sense of self is threatened, your emotions can feel so intense that your thoughts run out of control. You might say to yourself: *I'm a failure. I'm so stupid. Nobody will ever really love me.* It can feel like the earth is crumbling and you're going to fall through a giant crack. Thoughts are so powerful that sometimes all you can see is obstacles, and giving up seems the only option.

Buddhist psychology points to our beliefs and how tightly we hold onto them as the cause of mental suffering. Getting rid of thoughts is not the solution, however. Rather, the solution is learning how to see thoughts skillfully (Kornfield 2008, 146–147). When you see thoughts as "mental formations," they're like feathers that float away in the wind, bubbles that rise in water and dissolve at the surface, or clouds that change and move across the sky. By letting go of your clinging, you can witness your thoughts as events rather than facts and not have them define who you are.

The story of Buddha and the arrows demonstrates the role of thoughts in suffering: Buddha asked his students, "How would you feel if you were struck by an arrow?"

"Oh, that would really hurt," responded the students.

"How would you feel if struck by a second arrow?" inquired Buddha.

"Oh, much worse; it would be terrible!" they replied.

Buddha explained to them that being struck by an arrow would indeed produce unavoidable suffering, but negative self-talk about having been wounded—for example: *If only I had been more careful! What if I never walk again?*—would be like being struck by a second arrow. This is called "optional suffering" (Fronsdal 2001, 53–54).

According to the ancient Greek philosopher Epictetus, "We are disturbed not by what happens to us, but by our thoughts about what happens" (Mitchell 2009, 149). Our thoughts tend to distort reality in various ways. Cognitive therapy refers to this as cognitive distortion. David Burns, MD, bestselling author of the book *Feeling Good: The New Mood Therapy*, popularized cognitive therapy. To treat mood disorders and raise self-esteem, he identified ten cognitive distortions, including the following (Burns 1980, 42–43):

- All-or-nothing thinking/overgeneralizing

- Obsessing over the negatives, dismissing the positives

- Expanding things out of proportion or shrinking their importance

- Jumping to conclusions and reasoning based on feelings

- Criticizing yourself with "shoulds," "shouldn'ts," "musts," and "have tos"

- Labeling yourself as a bad or flawed person rather than declaring that you've made a mistake

Mindfulness places attention on actual experiences, free of distortions. "Mindfulness itself is the ultimate frame within which to perceive the actuality of things as they are" (Kabat-Zinn 1990, 331). If mindfulness is the ultimate frame, mindful self-esteem might be defined as "self reframed."

TRY THIS

A curious way to experience the power of thoughts is by returning to the yoga exercise you learned in step 10. Begin by standing tall and balanced in mountain pose. Spread your arms wide like a bird and slowly swan dive toward the floor as you bend forward at your waist with a flat back. Release into this folding stretch as you're hanging in rag doll pose.

1. For thirty seconds, without straining to bend further or feeling excessive discomfort, flood yourself with unwholesome messages or cognitive distortions that lead to feelings of negativity—for example: *I wish I weren't so stiff; I can't wait until this pose is over; There's nothing I can do to not feel tight; This exercise is a waste of time.*

2. Gently roll up, one vertebra at a time, until you're standing once again in mountain pose. Take a few moments to note the consequences of these unwholesome thoughts for how you felt emotionally and physically.

3. Spread your arms wide like a bird and slowly swan dive toward the floor. For thirty seconds again, hang in rag doll pose, without straining to bend further or feeling excessive discomfort. Fuel yourself with wholesome messages or cognitive reframings that lead to feelings of positivity—for example: *I can breathe through the discomfort; I can focus on the out-breath, the "letting go" breath; I can relax into the stretch; I will learn something important here.*

4. Gently roll up, one vertebra at a time, until you're standing again in mountain pose. Take a few moments to note the consequences of these wholesome thoughts for how you felt emotionally and physically.

Were you able to feel the difference in your level of emotional disturbance, physical discomfort, or stretching ability when flooding yourself with unwholesome thoughts (cognitive distortions) versus when fueling yourself with wholesome thoughts (cognitive reframings) that accepted this exercise for what it is—just an exercise?

25. Pain Times Resistance Equals Suffering

One of our main misperceptions is that life should be a kind of Shangri-la, free from strife. When life proves otherwise (because this is what life does), we resist. We might say to ourselves: *Why is this happening to me? This isn't fair! This is too hard; I hate it!* We then engage in a futile attempt to rearrange the world. This is *dukkha*, one of Buddha's three basic truths of existence—suffering or dissatisfaction caused by wanting things to be different from how they actually are; clinging to what you want as if you could stop what you don't want to happen from happening.

We orient our lives around these conditioned pursuits of happiness, attempting to fix what's happening before it falls apart and changes again. However, this only causes more angst. Steven Hayes, founder of acceptance and commitment therapy (ACT), says it like this: "As a rule, trying to get rid of your pain only amplifies it, entangles you further in it, and transforms it into something traumatic" (Hayes 2008, 7). Put succinctly, it's your resistance to what's happening that's the problem. This fundamental teaching of Buddha has been put into a mathematical equation by American Vipassana meditation teacher Shinzen Young (2004, 84):

Pain times Resistance equals Suffering

If resistance is the reason for suffering, what's the way out of suffering? Buddha points to its polar opposite—acceptance: "being with" what is; seeing things, in the present moment, as they truly are—not as how you wish they were.

Acceptance

Acceptance is a state of open receptivity, a willingness to invite in even the most unwelcome guests, and an ability to turn toward that which you resist. The more you embrace suffering and come to know it, the less you're compulsively driven by avoiding it. You experience a certain "lightness of being." Paradoxically, you move toward discomfort, rather than away, to break free.

This same paradoxical approach pertains to escaping the force of a powerful waterfall that holds you underwater. Instead of fighting against it to swim up to the surface, you dive into the depths, away from its invincible power. Once out from its hold, you can swim up to a different spot. Acceptance doesn't mean having a passive attitude or relinquishing your values so that, for example, you believe that there's nothing you can do about serious injustices. It simply means not resisting, accepting what's actually happening, and seeing things as they are. Acceptance isn't something to strive for. "Trying" to accept can add yet another level of suffering, because once again you're trying to get somewhere other than where you are.

TRY THIS

Notice your resistance. You're resisting whenever you're trying too hard, fighting against what's happening, or ignoring what's happening altogether. Are you struggling to lose weight, racing down the street before the light turns red, or procrastinating on that dreaded task of paying bills? How do you notice resistance in your thinking, how does resistance influence your emotions, and how does resistance feel in your body? Next, notice what happens when you turn toward resistance with acceptance. What thoughts are connected to acceptance, what emotions result from acceptance, and how does acceptance feel in your body? Write what you've learned in a journal entry.

26. Turn to Look

When you constantly seek the comfort of a sense of control, you try to impose your will on the world. Your mind is seduced into an endless loop of judging, obsessing, planning, fantasizing, and rehearsing that keeps you stuck in "doing" mode. This depletes your energy.

Conversely, when you're in "being" mode, you face reality as it is. This means that you can rest in awareness itself, in the present moment. Relaxing into the moment creates a space for you to unhinge from your conditioned reflex of control, fear, and vigilance. In this space, you find two basic choices: to "be with" what's happening (acceptance) or to fight against what's happening (resistance). If you want to liberate yourself from suffering, you must paradoxically give way to it.

Every time you feel distress, ask yourself, *What's this suffering?* Turn to look at it. Come to know it. When you see it clearly, your suffering begins to fade away.

TRY THIS

Work with resistance in your meditation practice. Even though you probably feel so much better after meditating and realize its benefits, you're not alone if you're coming face-to-face with resistance: believing that there's a right way and a wrong way to meditate; thinking you're not getting enough out of meditation; trying too hard and getting diminishing returns; sitting for only five minutes when you had intended to sit for twenty; feeling as if you don't have time to meditate; or giving up altogether. The habit of exerting control over life is so strong, letting go of "doing" can feel unfamiliar and threatening.

For whatever reason, when you're not following through on your intention to meditate, recognize this as resistance and then come to know it by informally using resistance as your "object of attention" (adapted from Bodhipaksa 2009). Turn toward resistance to learn what it's telling you. Explore your *relationship* with it in your emotions, physical sensations, and energy. Is there a sense of anxiety? Guilt? Agitation? Frustration? Is there physical tightness or tension? Trembling? Numbness? Do you feel dull or tired, or do you feel rushed? What insights emerge? Do you feel as though you need to stay busy to escape from inner turmoil? Do you not deserve to take care of yourself? Are you afraid of being a phony? Are you worried that if you begin meditating and stop again, you'll continue to feel greater and greater failure and trust yourself less and less? As you open the door to resistance, greet it as your ally or friend. Review the suggestions on establishing a meditation practice in the foundation section of this book. Remember, there's no right way or wrong way, no success or failure, in meditating. Just allow yourself to get curious.

27. Get to Know It

All too often, when you react to situations and circumstances that seem to appear out of nowhere and take on a power of their own, you're caught in the force of habit: an ingrained pattern of reacting that has become your default mode of operation. The longer and more often you engage in a habit, the stronger it becomes. What's more, efforts to force yourself to stop a habit often ultimately backfire. It's like trying to get your car out of the mud: the harder you step on the gas pedal, the faster your wheels spin, the deeper the track, and the more trapped you become.

Habits reside in your thoughts and emotions, the way you relate to your body, your behavior, and your actions. Many of your habits are unconscious, having formed when you were very young and having been learned in the environment in which you were raised. These mindless habitual patterns put a mask over your eyes so you can't see things as they truly are. Each of us, to a greater or lesser extent, is a creature of habit.

Sometimes your habitual thoughts are so intrusive during meditation that staying with the "object of attention" is just about impossible. This is when exploring and "working with" thoughts in meditation is a helpful course of action. Most likely, there's something about these thoughts that's important to understand.

Instead of judging your thoughts as positive, negative, or inappropriate, simply make room for whatever thoughts arise, without holding tightly to them or, alternatively, running from them. Rather than identifying with your thoughts, stand back and observe them as nonpersonal events—experiences arising out of conditions and then passing away. When you distance yourself from your thoughts in this way, you don't get so caught up in them. This permits you to see the whole story. You may begin to pick up familiar repetitious thought patterns, or "tapes." For example, when judging yourself for thinking *I'll never find what I'm looking for*, you might affix the light-hearted label "Searching for Shangri-la." Ask yourself: *Where does this thought come from? Is it really true? What would I be like without this thought?* Notice how the stories you weave are based on false assumptions. With a spirit of friendly curiosity, look into how you're habitually relating to this thought.

- What *emotion* is fueling the thought—fear, doubt, sadness? Feeling worthless may be a real trigger in your story line. If you find yourself rehearsing the future, this is often stimulated by feelings of anxiety or fear; rehashing the past is usually linked with feelings of guilt or shame. These emotions tend to wrap a cocoon around thoughts, encasing them in patterns of defeat.

- What *energy* is behind the thought? Are you clinging to the thought, resisting it, or denying it
  altogether?

- What *physical sensations* manifest—tightness in
  your chest, an aching head? How would you
  describe these sensations—hard or soft, big or
  little, light or dark? For example, when you feel
  burdened with responsibility, you may literally feel
  a weight on your shoulders, while with sadness or
  loss you may feel heaviness in your chest (a heavy
  heart). Telling yourself *It's okay to feel this...I can be
  with what is* helps soften the discomfort with
  acceptance (Goldstein 1993, 39).

Acknowledge the thought without repressing, judging,
or identifying with it. Loosen your identification with the
thought and say to yourself, *I am not my thought!* In a somewhat comic spirit, recognize the "Searching for Shangri-la"
tape and bid it be on its way.

TRY THIS

Tara Brach, psychologist and author of the pioneering
book *Radical Acceptance: Embracing Your Life with the
Heart of a Buddha*, popularized a way of investigating
thoughts in meditation through the acronym RAIN:
Recognize (name the thought), Accept (allow the thought),
Investigate (explore the thought in emotion, energy, and

physical sensations), and Non-identification (relate to the thought as a nonpersonal event) (Brach 2012, 61–75). These four elements are widely used to teach meditation on thoughts, but are not always identified in the same way.

The following meditation on thoughts emphasizes acceptance. Use it when a persistent, invasive thought arises during a meditative session. At any time, if the thought is too intense to stay with, you can always come back to your body or your breath to anchor yourself. You can then choose to return to the thought or not. If you'd like to listen to an audio version of this meditation, you may download one at www.newharbinger.com/27954.

Name the thought; name the tape. Use "mental noting." For example, note a thought about wishing things were different by saying to yourself, *This is fantasizing.* "Name the tape": label the familiar story or critical statement that keeps repeating itself behind the thought. For example, say to yourself, *This is "Lost Horizon."* Accept the thought for what it is: just a thought.

Observe and experience the thought as a nonpersonal event. Witness the thought as a "mental formation," an experience arising out of conditions and then fading away. Say to yourself, *I am not my thought.* Experience the thought with acceptance, allowing the thought to move through you as you neither cling to it nor push it away.

Explore the thought in your emotions, energy, and physical sensations. What emotion gives rise to the thought: what emotion is pushing the button for your tape to be played? Notice if you are running into the future or, alternatively, falling into the past, and notice what's driving these tendencies. What energy is fueling the thought? Is it clinging? Resistance? Denial? Explore how the emotion is expressing itself in your body. If you feel sadness, investigate the physical sense of sadness. Is it heavy? Dark? Dense? Sharp? Accept the experience with kindness. Rather than saying *I feel sad*, say, *This is what sadness feels like*. Tell yourself, *It's okay to feel this*. Notice whether the sensations shift location or change in any way.

When you're ready to end your exploration, return to your breath to anchor your attention, feeling the soft massage of the breath waves.

28. No Blame

Conditional self-esteem is based on approval: outside evaluations and outcomes that determine your worth. Mindful self-esteem, on the other hand, is based on self-acceptance: the ability to embrace all parts of yourself, without distinction. With mindful self-esteem, even though you recognize your limitations, that doesn't get in the way of unconditionally accepting who you are. Self-acceptance is transformative. Focusing on what's right or feeling optimistic is known to lead to a longer and healthier life than feeling pessimistic and worrying about things outside your control.

When you focus on what's wrong, you strive to fill the void in your desperate attempt to be okay. But when you focus on what's right, you start from the perspective that you accept yourself as you are, with all your inadequacies and imperfections. Curiously, it's not until you accept yourself for who you are that you're free to change. This is the paradox of self-acceptance and is at the forefront of understanding self-esteem from the perspective of mindfulness.

Resistance to the way things are and the misperception that you have a problem and need to be fixed leads you to desires and attachments. When you accept yourself regardless, you rid yourself of judgments, expectations, desires, and aversions. You appreciate, validate, and support who you are right now, even those parts of yourself that you would like to change. The realization that you're already whole comes from accepting that this very moment itself is perfect and complete as it is.

It's helpful to ask yourself where your lack of self-acceptance comes from. From a psychodynamic perspective, it probably began when you were young: Unconsciously, your parents or primary caregivers projected their hangups, such as their own issues of inadequacy, onto you by being critical, judgmental, or punitive. Unfortunately, they were often unable to separate *who* you were from *what* you did. As a child, too young to know any better, you fell victim to the emotional fallout. You then carried these beliefs about yourself into adult life, interpreting your very *self* as the problem. You internalized a self-esteem that was based not on how you're right or good, but on how you're wrong or bad.

Joseph Weiss, the founder of control mastery theory, refers to such early interpretations about yourself as "pathogenic beliefs" (Weiss 1986). You believe, for example, that you were uncared for because you were unlovable; you were devalued because you were inferior; or you were ignored because you were ugly. You then go about testing this theory to prove it wrong. But because you're more comfortable with what's familiar, paradoxically you go about proving it right! This only further perpetuates a damaged sense of self.

This is the legacy of a broken self-esteem: it's carried from one generation to the next. Knowing that you're part of a dysfunctional lineage of self-esteem connects you with our common humanity, enables you to feel closer to the whole of the human race, and frees you from blaming yourself for not meeting expectations that are primarily outside your control. Through your mindfulness practice, you can understand where your insecurities come from and how you get entangled in them. By inviting self-acceptance to emerge, you can break the damaged self-esteem that has bound generations.

TRY THIS

Through journaling, explore what you don't accept about yourself. Are you hard on yourself when you make mistakes? Do you regret decisions that have influenced the course of your life? Do you hang on to resentments toward others? Do you yearn for an intimate relationship but have difficulty committing, or, alternatively, have you stayed for too long in a relationship that's unhealthy? What judgments, expectations, desires, or limitations do you place on yourself? What are the costs?

Where did this lack of self-acceptance come from? Do you notice a familiar repetitious thought pattern, story line, critical message, or pathogenic belief that leaves you with feelings of worthlessness? Does it have roots in your childhood? Do its origins lie with a specific person, trau-matic event, or circumstance? Is this thought *really* valid or true? Can you feel the lineage of broken self-esteem passed down through the generations? Can you allow yourself to let go of your guilt and shame for failing to meet unrealistic needs and expectations? Can you forgive your-self for your lack of perfection?

29. The Unfolding Process

So much of what we do is driven by a desire for distraction from ourselves. Too often, we scramble to mask feelings of inadequacy and insecurity by engaging in compulsive activity. Though hurrying through the day with a sense of urgency is draining, it may feel less threatening than slowing down and coming face-to-face with yourself. You may get a kind of "rush" when you exert control and feel consumed by an approaching deadline, and a kind of "hush" when things get too quiet and there's a sense of something stirring.

From a need to take control and secure your position, you may attempt to find short-term fixes for lifelong issues. You may be driven to lock in a permanent, stable sense of self and a predictable, reliable life. This pattern of holding on to keep things stabilized is so pervasive, it's not so much life you fear, but the life you have to live. You fight against the second characteristic of existence: *anicca*, the reality that all things change and are by their very nature impermanent. Resisting the nature of *anicca* is indeed a losing battle.

Patience

Patience is the understanding that some situations unfold in their own time, outside of your control. When you accept each moment in its fullness, you let go of your defensive shield. You can meet yourself in your completeness and open to life's unfolding nature. In this way, you come to know the effortlessness and wisdom of patience.

Patience teaches that, paradoxically, "there is nothing that's permanent except impermanence—nothing remains without change" (Kung 2006, 5). Patience means experiencing life *in process* with an orientation on the present. It means slowing down and relaxing into the unfolding nature of life rather than hurrying to cross to-do items off your list. Patience is the ability to wait for an anticipated outcome, be tolerant of those slower than you, and be okay with your own failings without feeling anxious, irritable, or frustrated. It provides the strength, stability, and courage to stay—just stay.

Patience creates a space to disengage from your habitual compulsive reacting so you have the choice to respond differently. With more room to operate, you can step back and gain perspective. Patience is a true asset to a mindfulness practice, providing perseverance when doubt, disillusionment, or anxiety would otherwise get in your way.

TRY THIS

One way to develop patience is by coming to know impatience. Sit down to meditate for five minutes specifically during a time of day you're normally busy. Purposely use impatience as your "object of attention." Watch impatience with the intention of not acting on it—in other words, with patience.

- Notice what *thoughts* are associated with impatience. Are you concerned you're not doing something more important, or that you're not planning or rehearsing what you're going to do next?

- Notice what *emotions* are tied to impatience. Do you feel irritation, anger, boredom, or resentment?

- Notice how you hold impatience in your *body*. Do you fidget, tense your shoulders, or clench your jaw?

Rather than trying to get rid of impatience, blame yourself for feeling this way, or justify it, "work with" impatience with a willingness to be where you are when wishing you were somewhere else. This relaxes your mind and creates a space to be receptive to the present moment and open to the experience of being you.

30. The Buddha Within

A key principle of Buddhist psychology is to recognize original goodness and remember that your essential nature is good and pure. This inherent worth, your "Buddha nature," has always existed in you and will never leave. When you trust yourself, you realize that in this very moment we are all Buddhas. Mindful self-esteem is recognizing the Buddha within!

Trust as Self-Reliance

Trust as self-reliance means trusting yourself and your feelings rather than looking outside yourself for what's true. It means honoring and taking full personal responsibility for your feelings and intuitions and having the willingness to make mistakes along the way. It means believing in your inner wisdom. When you operate from a place of trust, your understanding of yourself comes from your own direct experience rather than through concepts or constructs as taught by others.

Trust in your basic goodness is a willingness to experience all of yourself—including the unworthiness that you feel in your thoughts, your emotions, and your body. This ability to open to all of it leads to the realization that your thoughts and feelings don't constitute your identity; they're in constant flux.

Your ego—your assumptions and beliefs about who you are—covers up your original goodness. It keeps you from recognizing your dynamic, changing nature. When you let go of the need to identify with your experiences, you see the nature of your experiences as impersonal; you see them as they naturally unfold. When you accept the three truths of reality—*dukkha* (dissatisfaction), *anicca* (impermanence), and *anatta* (egolessness)—you bring your suffering to an end.

In the ancient Chinese text *Tao Te Ching*, Lao-tzu eloquently puts forth this paradox: "When I let go of what I am, I become what I might be" (1988, *Tao Te Ching* No. 15). By letting go of the story that defines, limits, and separates you, you free yourself up to be more of your authentic self and part of the greater whole.

TRY THIS

Part of the following exercise is an adaptation of an exercise on resilience taught by Anna Douglas and Laura Vanett at Spirit Rock Retreat Center in Woodacre, California. Look back into your near or distant past, to a time when you met a difficult situation with a quality that fostered a sense of trust, confidence, or appreciation in yourself. You might reflect on a situation that was brief and sudden or, alternatively, one that lasted many months and changed over time. Perhaps you learned perseverance, courage, or resourcefulness as you met the challenge. Perhaps it was this very quality that helped guide your actions, like your personal North Star. Put yourself back in this difficult situation as though it were happening right now, with your central focus on this quality.

In what way does this quality serve as a valued resource, bringing the gift of confidence or trust as self-reliance? Acknowledge yourself at this time not as a fixed identity, such as a widow (if reflecting on the passing of your husband) or sick person (if reflecting on an illness), but rather a quality that shaped your actions and intentions and enabled you to relate to what was happening and be present in a certain way. Recognize this gift of presence as something present within you right now and always.

Now consider what sort of commonplace object or shape would best represent this quality. Steadfastness might be represented by a rock; kindness, by a heart; courage, by an arrowhead. Find an object that represents this quality to you, and keep it handy as a reminder of your basic goodness, the Buddha within!

PART 3

EMOTIONS AND THE HEART

In part 2, you practiced moving toward painful thoughts with mindful awareness and self-acceptance. Now, in part 3, you'll learn to embrace painful emotions with self-compassion. Atop the "seven pillars" of mindfulness is what Buddhism refers to as the "crown jewel" of compassion. Surrounding this precious heart stone are the gems of openness, equanimity, loving-kindness, gratitude, sympathetic joy, and generosity.

Born of ever-changing conditions, emotions, like thoughts, arise and pass. In the arms of compassion, you can hold your hurting self-esteem and send yourself sympathy and support. Being held in this way fills you with energy to engage with the world not just for your own good, but for the good of others and all you encounter.

31. Spaciousness

Our propensity is to categorize emotions as positive or negative. But emotions, like thoughts, are not intrinsically good or bad. They can, however, become destructive if you resist them—that is, if you judge them, try to control them, obsess over them, or push them away. Anger, for example, may lead to resentment. Fear may become basic insecurity.

Buddhist psychology refers to emotional states as either "wholesome" or "unwholesome." Its intention is to "work with" emotions through focused attention, not get rid of them. As with distressing thoughts, mindfulness teaches you to turn toward painful emotions in order to break free of them.

Openness

Mindfulness sets the conditions for your heart to become spacious—able to hold, feel, and release any and all emotions. Openness is a wide, receptive, accepting state, a state that can contain all things. It's free from self-effort and agendas and allows all emotions to be present, making room for options to emerge and compassion to arise. Being open doesn't necessarily mean being emotionally expressive, as the phrase is sometimes used. Rather, it means that you allow emotions to move through your heart without holding on to them tightly or, alternatively, trying to force them away. How do you do this? You create space for them to be.

One of the five main scriptures on the teachings of Buddha, the Anguttara Nikaya, uses the analogy of salt in water to explain how the practice of mindfulness helps you receive and hold difficult experiences (Bhikkhu 2012, A. III, 99): If a tablespoon of salt is added to a cup of water, the water will taste really salty. But if the same tablespoon of salt is added to a gallon of water, the water will taste less salty. If the same tablespoon of salt is added to a pond, its taste is further diluted. Like salt in a pond, painful emotions dissolve in a spacious mind and an open heart.

TRY THIS

For the following experiment, you need a clear shot glass (or other small glass); a clear pint size mug (or other large glass); and a vial of food coloring.

Fill each glass with water, and then add one drop of food coloring to each. Watch the water take on a hue as the food coloring dissolves. Stir the water so the color is evenly distributed, then observe the difference in intensity of hue in each glass. Notice how you can see through the large glass but not the small one.

When you look at the deep, dark, dense color in the shot glass, this is the intensity of unwholesome emotions that are so concentrated; all you see is its strength. There's no way to see past the strong emotions or to not feel consumed by them. When you look at the almost clear, translucent touch of color in the pint mug, this is the gentleness of wholesome emotions that become soft when you give them room and allow compassion to arise. The ability to clearly see through this spacious container to the other side leads to understanding the options that lie ahead.

32. The Forces of Mara

We tend to see distressing emotions not only as negative but, worse yet, as our enemies. As with thoughts, how you view your emotions depends on how you *relate* to them. When you're in the throes of despairing emotions, do you harden around them and shut down, or do you soften to them and open up? Can you learn from what your emotions are telling you?

Your propensity to avoid pain may cause you to see distress as an obstacle. The need for comfort and security fuels this compulsion and seduces you into seeing avoidance of pain as a legitimate need, even when it means feeling worse or going numb.

In stories about Buddha, there is a demon or nuisance named Mara who uses deception, attack, and disguise to create fear and confusion or try to tempt Buddha away from the spiritual life. In the story of one attempt to keep Buddha from enlightenment, Mara sends his three beautiful daughters (representing thirst, desire, and delight) to seduce Buddha. In another attempt, Mara sends his army to throw deadly weapons at Buddha.

Yet in his many fabled encounters with the different forces of Mara, Buddha manages to perceive the demon not as an enemy but as a friend. Rather than seeing Mara as throwing obstacles in his way, Buddha sees these situations as tests that bring him insight into the nature of life and the ways of getting trapped (Chödrön 2000, 65).

There are said to be four forms of Mara, one of which is the Mara of emotion. This Mara personifies the illusory force that comes to spin you into doubt and confusion, deplete your confidence, and steal your "basic wisdom mind"—the inherent truth of your natural goodness. Mara shows how strong emotions can lure you into delusion through weaving your thoughts into stories. These stories are so compelling they yank you into their vortex and take on a power of their own (Chödrön 2000, 69). For example, every time you feel dismissed and minimized by your husband, you believe it's because he doesn't value your opinions or insights. Whatever anger you unload whenever you feel this way feels justified because, once again, you've been wronged. You hold more tightly to the "truth" and power of the story than to the "truth" of your basic goodness. You may also hold more tightly to the belief that your husband doesn't have good intentions, or that he means to imply your opinions and insights aren't valuable than to the "truth" of his basic goodness!

Every time you notice a need to avoid suffering by shutting down and losing touch with yourself, you can use the quality of openness to "be with" what's inside—your fears, faults, and failures. You can open and soften to your emotions and then send Mara on his way. As it says in the great Buddhist scripture the Dhammapada: "Those who enter the path, and practice meditation, are released from the bondage of Mara" (Boyd 1975, 124).

TRY THIS

Name an emotion that you sometimes feel so strongly it sends you into a swirl of doubt and confusion, drains your confidence, and washes away your basic wisdom. If you imagine this emotion as Mara, what does he look like? Is he fear, cloaked as a monster who comes to devour? Is he confusion, masquerading as a trickster who distorts the truth? Is he depression, disguised as a potion to dull your senses? Is he anger, concealed as spears and daggers? When tempted by Mara, your "enemy," how do you harden around him and shut down? When you're afraid, do you become passive and weak? When you're confused, do you become scattered and anxious? When you're depressed, do you become withdrawn and rundown? When you're angry, do you become blaming and hostile? When visited by Mara, your "teacher," how can you soften to him and open up to learn from what he's telling you? Are you afraid because you're scared to fail (or maybe succeed); confused because you keep yourself busy to avoid your feelings; depressed because you don't deserve to be happy; or angry because you feel like a bad person and blame yourself for not being perfect? What do you need that you're not giving yourself—forgiveness? Understanding? Attention? Fun? Creativity? Curiosity?

Draw a picture of a powerful, unwholesome emotion as the illusory force of Mara. Invite Mara to attack in his best disguise, with great force or cunning seduction! Use vivid colors, heavy lines, and jagged edges. When you're done, complete the following sentences and write them beneath your picture:

- When Mara is my enemy, I shut down by...

- When Mara is my teacher, this is what I understand...

- This is what I need...

May you always be transformed by the presence of Mara!

33. Explore the Container

How do you cultivate openness to work with your emotions in meditation? When in meditation and you feel the presence of an emotion, recognize this as the Mara of emotion: meet him head on and with your heart open. To have the courage to not run from the emotion, give yourself permission to not always have pleasant emotions. To stay with the emotion, relax into it—feel it gently. Say to yourself, *It's okay to feel whatever's here to feel.* To see the emotion as a challenge or friend, rather than an obstacle or enemy, learn what it's telling you. To not identify with the emotion, rest in the spacious container of your mind, where your Buddha within resides.

In the book *Focused and Fearless*, Insight meditation teacher Shaila Catherine (2008, 66–67) discusses emotions as a fluctuating, dynamic process and suggests that if you don't refuel them with obsessive thinking, they'll simply run out of gas: "The Buddha described a human being as a guesthouse; many kinds of feelings come, stay for a while, and then travel on. Try greeting all emotions as visitors or guests. Allow them to visit, accept that they arise due to conditions, but don't adopt them as permanent residents" (Catherine 2008, 67).

TRY THIS

An audio version of this meditation is available at www .newharbinger.com/27954.

Similar to the meditation in which you investigated thoughts (step 27), this meditation investigates emotions. It too is an adaptation of the four-step practice best known as RAIN: Recognize, Allow, Investigate, and Non-identification (widely taught by Tara Brach).

Enter into the present moment by bringing your attention to your breath and body sensations and your intention to be fully present. Look at yourself with your mind's eye as if from a distance, witnessing yourself sitting. When a powerful emotion arises, recognize this as Mara. Know that at any time, if the emotion is too intense to "be with," you can return to your body and your breath to anchor yourself. You can then choose to return to the emotion or not.

Recognize the Mara of emotion. Without clinging to or, alternatively, avoiding the emotion, and without trying to explore why you feel the way you do, identify the emotion through "mental noting." Say to yourself, *This is* [*sadness*].

Hold Mara in openness. Give yourself permission to feel the emotion. Say to yourself, *It's okay to feel* [*sadness*]. Call upon your courage to turn toward the emotion, giving it space so it can move through you. Say to yourself, *I can be with this feeling.*

Learn what Mara is telling you. Ask yourself, *What is [sadness]?* Do you carry this emotion as a knot in your stomach or a trembling in your hands? Do you hold on to a critical statement that induces guilt or shame? Do you want to run from, attach to, minimize, or deny the emotion?

See Mara as a delusion. Rather than identifying with the emotion as "yours," observe it as a nonpersonal event arising out of conditions and then passing away. Relax into the state of openness, into your "Buddha nature."

34. A Place of Balance

Our tendency to glom onto pleasant feelings, push away unpleasant ones, or choose indifference stimulates what's known in Buddhist psychology as the "three poisons": greed (from clinging), hatred (from aversion), and delusion (from indifference). These "poisons" are based on wanting to permanently feel the "joys" of pleasure, gain, praise, and fame and avoid the "sorrows" of their opposites: pain, loss, blame, and disrepute.

These "joys" and "sorrows" are particularly vulnerable to a self-esteem based on external measures of happiness and success. When you're caught in the "sorrows," you may take it as a personal failure, as though it's your own fault. You ride on the emotional roller coaster of never-ending "joys and sorrows," with no means of getting off.

Buddhist psychology refers to these four joys and their opposites as the "eight vicissitudes" and recognizes them as natural and recurrent conditions of life. This is why, in the allegories of Buddha and the illusory force of Mara, Mara was always close at hand. While it's vital to care for yourself and try to be happy, at the same time it's critical to know that you can't always be happy. It's important to have desires that are wholesome, and at the same time it's essential to recognize that loss and disappointment are par for the course.

Equanimity

Equanimity is the spaciousness of a still and balanced mind, a mind that can weather life's ups and downs. With the balance of equanimity, you can "be with" what is, without trying to change it to fit your needs and expectations.

Equanimity makes you resistant to the "three poisons" of clinging, aversion, and indifference, and it helps you develop a healthy relationship with the paradox of joys and sorrows. When you step off the roller coaster of unstable self-esteem, you can be okay with how you feel, not take things so personally, and maintain a strong and stable sense of self.

Equanimity is one of the four "Brahma-viharas," "heavenly abodes," or "heart qualities." It frees your heart and provides the base for the other three "heart qualities": compassion, loving-kindness, and sympathetic joy. Equanimity gives rise to wisdom; to the truth of impermanence or the changing nature of things. With equanimity, you see how your suffering is linked to your drive to avoid the inherent instability and uncertainty of life. You learn the difference between love of comfort and love of well-being, so you can choose what's truly nourishing. You have the courage to engage and respond to what Taoists call "the ten thousand joys and the ten thousand sorrows."

TRY THIS

Tibetan Buddhist monks practice the ritual art of sand painting, a form of "art meditation." They spend hours, days, or weeks meticulously placing grains of different colored sand, one at a time, into an intricate mandala design (a symbol of the universe) measuring several square feet. Once the work is complete, in a lesson of impermanence, they sweep the sand away!

Go to an art supply store and buy a sand mandala kit, or find one online. Another option is to get your own sand, pebbles, beads, or any kind of material or small objects to form into your own unique creative design. As you carefully craft your masterpiece, be open to your experience— whether it's pleasant or unpleasant. When you experience any aspect of this art project as an obstacle, meet it as a challenge. Without identifying with what you're feeling, stay with your emotion and get to know what's yanking you off balance or tossing you around. For example, if you realize that you've been using green sand when you were supposed to be using purple sand, get to know your frustration. If you think that the project is taking too long, get to know your impatience. Notice how expectations get in your way when you cling to a certain outcome (such as wanting the finished product to look perfect), dislike yourself for not having greater ability, or feel indifference or boredom. How you relate to this exercise provides insight into ways you cling (greed), avoid (hatred), and are indifferent (delusion).

When you place the final grain of sand (or pebble, bead, etc.), note how you feel. Before you brush it all away, note how you feel as you're about to destroy your work of art. Note how you feel as you watch it disappear and after it's all gone. Are you aware of the push and pull of pleasure and pain; gain and loss; and the other "joys and sorrows" that come your way? Can you hold the "eight vicissitudes" with equanimity?

35. Interweave

Your quest for conditional self-esteem has likely been a lonely one because of a focus on yourself: the belief that *you* are the only one who suffers with *your* issues. It's easy to take things personally when everything seems to be happening to *you*. But when you step back with the spacious, still, and balanced mind of equanimity, you notice that emotions, like thoughts, aren't really *yours* but arise and pass away out of causes and conditions. The emotions and thoughts that you experience don't essentially belong to you; you don't "own" them.

Thich Nhat Hanh (1992) coined the term "interbeing" to reflect the interrelated nature of all things. He gives the example of looking deeply into a sheet of paper you're reading from. He points out that if it weren't for clouds, there would be no rain; if it weren't for rain, no trees could grow; if it weren't for trees, paper couldn't be made. He goes on to say that if you continue to look even more deeply you can see the sunshine, the forest, the mill, the lumberjack, the lumberjack's parents, and even yourself—because looking at the paper is part of your perception. According to Nhat Hanh, everything is within this sheet of paper (Nhat Hanh 1992, 95–96).

We all are a part of an interconnected web—a relationship of interwoven conditions between everything that exists. When you understand the "interbeing" nature of all things, you realize that you have no truly separate "self." As you let go of your ego and its shortcomings, you recognize how you're part of the same fabric as everyone else. We all struggle to hold together at the seams while dealing with issues of inadequacy and insecurity. You understand that you're only human and that this struggle is part of the human condition.

From the wisdom of impermanence, the ever-changing nature of all things, and "interbeing"—the interwoven fluctuation of experience—you move beyond the limitation of a separate "self" into the spacious interconnection of "selflessness." You let down your guard and connect to life and the whole of the human race. You can then touch the "original goodness" that has always been within you and respond with compassion.

TRY THIS

Choose an object—something living or something manufactured, something big or something small, something edible or something usable—and look deeply into it as Nhat Hanh suggests. Trace the object back in time; delve into its history to the cause-and-effect relationship that brought this object into "interbeing."

After you've looked deeply into your chosen object, ask yourself, *Is it I who am looking at this object, or is it this object that is looking at me?*

36. Tend and Befriend

Our inability to distinguish between physical and emotional danger (see step 1), combined with our disposition to focus on the negative and interpret things we don't like as a personal assault, stimulates the "fight, flight, or freeze" response. But why is the brain this reactive, and what are the emotional consequences of being so defensive?

For humans, survival depends on being sensitively tuned to negative information in order for the "fight, flight, or freeze" response to function in the presence of threat (Neff 2011, 110–11). In the book *Buddha's Brain*, neuropsychologist Rick Hanson (2009) describes the brain as "negativity biased" to such a degree that negative experiences stick to the brain like Velcro and positive ones slide off like Teflon. From this underlying need to be safe, which also includes emotional safety, we minimize the positive and ruminate on the negative.

Fortunately the "fight, flight, or freeze" response (the stress response) is balanced by the "rest and digest" response (the relaxation response). But to our further benefit is what the leading scientific expert on self-compassion, Kristin Neff, explains in her groundbreaking book *Self-Compassion* (2011, 44): the "tend and befriend" response, or our instinctive nature to protect our offspring and give and receive nurturance. The neurotransmitter oxytocin, "the hormone of love and bonding," provides a sense of security and warmth, calms emotional distress, and stimulates this response. Neff asserts that our inherent biological nature demonstrates that "our brains are actually designed to care."

In *The Mindful Path to Self-Compassion*, notable psychologist Christopher Germer (2009, 3) discusses how the physiological reactions of your "fight, flight, or freeze" response are translated into how you feel about yourself. He describes how the fight response stimulates you to become self-critical; the flight response, to become emotionally withdrawn; and the freeze response, to become self-absorbed. But self-criticism, self-isolation, and self-absorption—the "unholy trinity," as Germer refers to it—can be put to rest in the embrace of self-compassion.

Self-Compassion

Self-compassion means caring for yourself in the same way you would care for someone you love. You can easily see your natural, innate self-compassion in how you hold your head when you have a headache or how you hug yourself when you cry. It softens the impact of negative events and lessens your tendency to obsess when you're feeling bad about yourself. When you allow self-compassion to flow, such emotions as hatred, anger, and resentment wash away.

Neff (2011) describes self-compassion as consisting of three central elements: (1) self-kindness—being gentle and understanding with yourself versus critical and judgmental; (2) acknowledgment of our common humanity—feeling connected to others versus isolated and alienated by your suffering; and (3) mindfulness—holding your experiences in balanced awareness versus feeling overwhelmed or avoiding pain. She demonstrates how self-compassion, unlike conditional self-esteem, is accessible when you're most vulnerable to feelings of inadequacy or failure and is a particularly stable way to regulate emotion, protecting you from the need to build yourself up when you're down. Neff views self-compassion as a better alternative to self-esteem, and most psychologists agree.

Self-compassion takes the "stick" out of Velcro and puts the "stay" into Teflon, rewiring the brain from being negatively biased to being positively biased. When you add the warmth of compassion to the wakefulness of awareness, deep change is possible. You can witness your unfolding nature and nurture its growth.

TRY THIS

There are different ways to stimulate the "tend and befriend" response. Here are a few.

Hug. Even when you don't have someone handy to hug, you're always available to hug yourself. Especially when you're feeling down or need to be soothed, give yourself a great big hug. Even crossing your arms over your chest while sitting in the office or walking down the street can help. Try hugging a pillow, a stuffed animal, or a tree. Neff (2011, 49) includes a hugging practice as one of her exercises to release oxytocin.

Pet an animal. Petting a dog, for example, is known to release oxytocin both in the dog and in the human (Zak 2008). Hold the animal on your lap, or snuggle up close and make eye contact, feeling every stroke, paying attention to the texture of the fur. Don't minimize the value of petting any animal you love or those you may meet when out for a walk, at a friend's home, or at an animal shelter.

Treat yourself to a massage. Massage has been shown to prime the brain to release oxytocin (Zak 2008). Visit a massage therapist; ask your partner for a nice, relaxing rubdown; or tackle those areas that you can reach yourself. You can always knead your own shoulders, rub your head, or roll your back on a tennis ball. All the while, breathe deeply.

Smile. Smiling has been shown to reduce stress and help people recover from stressful situations (Peterson 2012). Whether you're meditating or moving through the day, remember the "half smile" or "Buddha smile" (see step 9). A small, relaxed upturning of your mouth can have a big effect in lifting your heart and lightening your spirit. As

Thich Nhat Hanh is widely reported to have said, "Sometimes your joy is the source of your smile, but sometimes your smile can be the source of your joy."

As you stimulate your "tend and befriend" response by hugging, petting an animal, getting a massage, or smiling, you're also training your brain to be less negative and more positive!

37. Plant Your Garden

The quest for conditional self-esteem is a quest for a permanent stamp of approval that defends against failure. Conversely, self-compassion recognizes that success and failure arise and pass. Knowing that these things aren't connected to your value or worth enables you to better stay with your experiences (Neff 2011).

The need to be better than Suzy in the next office or Harold in upper Manhattan only causes you to feel separate and alone and perpetuates a need to defend against or be better than others. In order to build mindful self-esteem, you need to let yourself off the hook for not being better, bigger, brighter, or bolder—even though you're really not to blame.

When you have self-compassion, you know that you're deserving of love just as you are. Research shows that self-compassion honors both your strengths and your weaknesses, is stable in response to either praise or blame, and enables you to be open and undefended, because it embraces the reality that we're all in this together and suffering is part of our common humanity (Neff, Rude, and Kirkpatrick 2007). Self-compassion allows you to let go and relax, shed your armor, and explore your unfolding nature. Neff interprets self-compassion as a "way of relating to the mystery of who we are" (Neff 2011, 152).

Just as the seeds a gardener chooses determine the plants that grow, in Buddhist psychology, your future well-being is influenced by the intentions you nurture. Planting seeds of intention with guilt and remorse grows feelings of shame, while planting seeds of intention with love and acceptance grows forgiveness and compassion.

In each and every moment, you can choose what kind of seeds to plant. Whether your garden runs wild with thorny bushes or blooms with radiant flowers is up to you. Do you choose to fortify your armor with self-defense or heal your scars with self-compassion? Do you choose to manicure the garden so it looks perfect, or simply tend to it and watch it grow?

TRY THIS

In her mindfulness of emotions class, Renée Burgard instructs students to write qualities they wish to cultivate on large, uncooked white lima beans. The students place the beans in clear containers and watch them sprout. The following exercise underlines the cause-and-effect relationship between intention and outcome when planting "seeds of compassion." For this exercise, you need a patch of earth or dirt in a flowerpot.

Select seeds, bulbs, plant cuttings, or starter plants whose flowers will serve as a symbol of special importance or meaning to you. Perhaps they're wildflower seeds that you toss or sprinkle, whose abundant flowers wave freedom, creativity, and joy in the wind. Possibly it's a lily of the valley bulb, a reminder of your sweetness, humility, and returning happiness. Maybe it's the stalk of a geranium, because all that's required to grow this plant is that you stick it in the ground and water it from time to time. The geranium flower may be your symbol of not needing to strive so hard to be your already beautiful self. Perchance it's a little rose plant that will bloom red to signify passion, white to signify virtue, or yellow to signify friendship or devotion.

When you feast your eyes on the beautiful flower that your plant has sprouted, recognize this flower as the lovely person you are. If your plant doesn't sprout or bloom, this can still serve as a helpful exercise. It supports the need to care for your feelings with compassion. Explore changing the conditions: providing more or less water, moving the plant into an area of greater shade or more sunlight, replacing the soil, or, as referred to in mindfulness, "beginning anew"—in this case, using different seeds, bulbs, cuttings, or starter plants. Each time you keep coming back to your "seeds of intention," you're "tending and befriending" yourself with love and care.

38. Well-Wishing

Even though we may have twenty positive experiences and one negative experience during the course of a typical day, we typically zero in on the one negative experience. This means that we often lose sight of all our wonderful qualities when we perceive something negative about ourselves. Given this instinctual negative orientation, intentionally supporting the positive is truly essential.

Loving-Kindness

Loving-kindness means having intentions of well-wishing and the capacity to bring joy and happiness to yourself and others. When you wish yourself well, you're able to better hold difficult emotions. You "re-mind" yourself that you're already whole and complete and worthy of giving and receiving love.

In the West, the practice of loving-kindness has been greatly influenced by Sharon Salzberg, a leading Insight meditation teacher, and is beautifully taught in her seminal book, *Lovingkindness: The Revolutionary Art of Happiness*. Loving-kindness, or *metta*, is both a meditation and an informal mindfulness practice that you can sprinkle throughout your day. In the formal tradition of loving-kindness, you set your intentions by repeating four phrases, addressing five categories of people in turn.

Categories:

1. Yourself

2. A dear friend—someone you care about, such as a friend, family member, or teacher

3. A neutral person—someone you know personally or impersonally whom you feel neutral about

4. A difficult person—someone you have difficult feelings toward

5. All beings—every being throughout the world

Phrases:

1. "May _____ be safe."

2. "May _____ be healthy."

3. "May _____ be happy."

4. "May _____ live with ease of well-being."

Repeating these phrases helps you deeply internalize intentions of well-being. It breaks down the barriers between you and others and brings light into your heart. Through this practice, you can know the power of love. Throughout the day, wherever you are, connecting to intentions of kindness produces feelings of contentment.

The practice starts with sending well-wishes to yourself, but because our Western culture so inclines us to be self-critical, this can feel difficult to fully embrace. If so, start instead with the "dear friend" category to help you nurture feelings of positivity. Because every moment in the mind manifests in new intentions, every moment has the potential to generate acts of kindness and compassion. Over time, these "random acts of kindness" that you've sprinkled through the day grow into the person you become.

TRY THIS

The following loving-kindness meditation is based on the teachings of Shaila Catherine, founder and principal teacher at Insight Meditation South Bay (IMSB).

Take your seat to meditate, and close your eyes. Slow your breath, quiet your mind, and "drop into your heart"—look as if you're *seeing* from your heart. When you're settled, offer intentions of loving-kindness to yourself. With each breath, as you fill your heart with the following well-wishes, internalize them with ever greater sincerity:

- *May I be safe.*

- *May I be healthy.*

- *May I be happy.*

- *May I live with ease of well-being.*

Say the phrases not with the intention of creating an idyllic state, but instilling the wish to be free of suffering. If you prefer, add your own intentions or say these intentions in your own words. Notice when feelings of loving-kindness arise, so that you can increasingly connect the intentions with such feelings. It can be helpful to visualize whom you're sending intentions to—in this case, yourself. If it's difficult to feel loving-kindness toward yourself, start with the "dear friend" category. Try wearing a half-smile to lift your heart as you say the phrases silently. If opposite feelings to loving-kindness arise, such as anger or resentment, recognize these feelings are in your heart and being released. When difficult emotions arise, you can return to your breath to calm and center yourself or stay with these feelings and bring loving-kindness toward them too.

Focus your practice on sending intentions of kindness to yourself until you feel a sense of ease. Take all the time you need to absorb the beauty of this compassion practice. There's no reason to short-change yourself from being the giver and receiver of love. When you're ready, you can slowly progress by moving through all the categories of people: a dear friend, a neutral person, a difficult person, and all beings. This will, most probably, occur over many sittings. Sending intentions of kindness to someone you feel no affection for is not necessarily easy. Be gentle with yourself. Treating yourself with loving-kindness will provide the tenderness you need to extend loving-kindness to others. Over time, you'll develop ease in sending intentions of well-being to all.

39. Send and Receive

A way to care for and connect to others with genuine nobility is through the Tibetan Buddhist "heart-practice" called *tonglen*. Different from other mindfulness practices, *tonglen* takes *in* pain through breathing *in* the inevitable suffering of life experience and sends *out* happiness and pleasure through breathing *out* compassion to all beings. In the profound book *When Things Fall Apart*, American Buddhist nun Pema Chödrön beautifully explains the paradoxical practice of *tonglen* and ways to engage in this practice (2000, 93–97).

Tonglen is paradoxical in that it reverses the habitual tendency to resist what's unpleasant and seek what's pleasurable. It's a powerful practice to work with resistance to suffering—*dukkha*. It expands your ability to feel emotions, understand the causes of suffering, and embrace your experiences with openness. When you tear down your defensive barrier, you release unconditional acceptance and compassion for yourself and others.

Reducing attachment to yourself also reverses *anatta*—resistance to not having a permanent sense of self. Holding on to "me," "mine," and "I" feeds the delusion of being separate and shields your essential nature. *Tonglen* opens you up, connects you to a larger reality, and registers you as a resident of the world. It helps shift self-centeredness to selflessness, because it's a wish that all beings might be free of suffering and a practice for the benefit of all. When you feel your connection to others and wish for their happiness, you relate to yourself and the world like a bodhisattva—a compassionate being.

Tonglen is a formal meditative practice and also an informal practice that you can do any time or in any situation, for a few seconds or a few minutes, with your eyes open or closed. There are many ways to practice *tonglen*, and you may find some easier than others.

You can practice *tonglen* by breathing in the suffering of someone dear to you and wishing to help, then breathing out an offering to release whatever suffering that person is experiencing. You can breathe in your own suffering and that of others experiencing the same distress, then breathe out happiness, comfort, or relief to yourself and others. When you're experiencing happiness, you can breathe in suffering with the wish that everyone might be free of suffering and breathe out the wish that everyone might feel happiness. The practice of *tonglen* offers an invaluable support to the cultivation of mindful self-esteem.

TRY THIS

Pema Chödrön (2000, 96–97) outlines four stages to the formal practice of *tonglen*: resting the mind in openness;

working with the texture of suffering (e.g., a feeling of heat or heaviness); working with a personal situation (e.g., the suffering of someone you care about or the pain you and others like you are feeling); and widening the circle of pain you're taking in and relief you're sending out, to include even those you consider your enemies. The following practice draws from this model.

1. Rest your mind in a state of openness or stillness. When you've arrived at this sense of spaciousness, breathe in a feeling of heaviness, constriction, and darkness. Breathe out a feeling of buoyancy, openness, and light. With each in-breath, allow the darkness of suffering to deepen. With each out-breath, invite the light to brighten.

2. Breathe in whatever difficult emotion you're experiencing. It may be a sense of anxiety or insecurity, fear, or confusion. Breathe out a sense of confidence, wholeness, appreciation, or any form of relief for this suffering.

3. As you breathe in, slowly expand the pain you take in to include others who are experiencing the same pain. As you breathe out, send relief to others who are experiencing this pain.

40. What Am I Ignoring?

When you overidentify with success or failure or are too concerned with comparing yourself to others, you're primarily geared toward coping. You forget to appreciate the present moment and experience your whole self.

Gratitude

Gratitude is the acknowledgment of appreciation; the ability to notice what's right, regardless. It frees you from clinging to what you want, avoiding what you don't want, or being indifferent to what there is. With gratitude, you can recognize and engage in the wonder of life.

When life is going well, it's valuable to acknowledge what there is to appreciate. You can appreciate things both big and small—you can appreciate someone you love, or you can appreciate a butterfly outside your window. It's especially helpful to acknowledge what there is to appreciate when you feel burdened with responsibility or fraught with distress. Making simultaneous room for such opposites as happiness and sorrow, or beauty and ugliness, softens your heart and calms your soul, allowing compassion to arise.

Try This

To cultivate gratitude in your daily life, bring your attention to what you appreciate when feeling the four "joys" of pleasure, gain, praise, and fame. For example, when you feel pleasure in a task well done, acknowledge your hard work. When you experience gain through being rewarded for your services, recognize that you deserve appreciation. When you are praised for how you look, credit the care you give yourself. When you experience fame and respect, honor the virtues that guide you.

Also, bring your attention to what you're ignoring when you feel the four "sorrows" of pain, loss, blame, and disrepute. For example, when you feel pain from making a mistake, acknowledge what you did that was right. When you feel loss when hearing sad news, know that all is not lost. If you are blamed when scolded, recognize that this is the result of deflecting responsibility onto others. When you are not respected, know that you have mindfulness as a valuable resource.

Notice whether the practice of gratitude frees you from the "three poisons": greed (clinging), hatred (avoiding), and delusion (being indifferent).

41. Count Your Blessings

Robert Emmons, the leading expert on the psychology of gratitude, describes how gratitude has been found to have a direct impact on happiness and can improve the quality of both emotional and physical experiences. People who are grateful are happier, more hopeful, and more satisfied with their lives. They're also less materialistic and less jealous of others' success (Emmons 2007).

Of all the "heart qualities" to cultivate, gratitude is considered the easiest. It weakens the tendency to be critical of yourself, softening your heart and building your capacity for forgiveness and deservingness. It spurs you to action and selfless giving, which leads to generosity and increased joy. It takes you out of personal confinement and into a sense of belonging to the larger web of being (Moffitt 2002, 61).

Gratitude reminds you of the good fortune of being alive so you can rejoice in the simple appreciation of all you take for granted, most notably yourself. To emphasize the blessing of being alive, Buddha described it as rarer than a blind turtle finding a small hoop to stick its head through in the vastness of the ocean (Moffitt 2002, 61).

TRY THIS

In your journal, list the many ways you feel blessed. For example, acknowledge those who love you and show concern for you—both humans and animals. Give thanks for the food on your table, the house you live in, the earth you walk on, and the air you breathe. Give gratitude to those you respect, honor, cherish, or hold dear. Before you turn off the light to sleep, read over your journal entry and add to it anything else you feel grateful for. How lovely to count your blessings and bring gratitude into your dreams!

42. Delight for Others

Do you ever feel envy or jealousy in reaction to others' success, good fortune, happiness, or abilities? Do you ever take pleasure in others' misfortune? If so, this is not unusual, particularly in our competitive culture.

Yet humans are inherently social and cooperative by nature. Beginning in infancy and throughout life, we're responsive to smiles and expressions of happiness. It's possible to break out of our conditioned competitive streak and return to this natural instinct to care, of wishing happiness for all.

Sympathetic Joy

Joy means rejoicing in what is. Joy is freedom from regret, resentment, and blame. To experience joy is to recognize life's blessings. Sympathetic joy, or *mudita*, means being able to feel happiness in the circumstances, accomplishments, gifts, and good qualities of others. In the loving-kindness practice, you send wishes to alleviate suffering. In the practice of sympathetic joy, you send happiness for others' success and good fortune. Sympathetic joy is an antidote to feelings of inadequacy and, importantly, to emotions that block your ability to feel compassion, such as jealousy, envy, resentment, hatred, and boredom.

When you understand that happiness can be found only in what you share with others, not in what's "yours," self-centeredness dissolves. By operating from a vantage point of abundance (feeling as if there's enough to go around) rather than scarcity, you return to your innately social and cooperative nature. You feel closer to others, even those who seem to have more going for them than you do. Others' happiness becomes *your* happiness. As your field of sympathetic joy widens, your happiness grows and grows. Paradoxically, the very act of taking pleasure in someone else's happiness draws you closer to yourself. The more deeply you practice sympathetic joy, the more confident and secure you become in your own happiness, even when faced with difficulty and hardship.

Similar to loving-kindness, sympathetic joy is both an informal and a formal mindfulness practice and, in the Buddhist tradition, you repeat phrases to address different categories of people.

Categories:

1. A benefactor—someone you feel grateful toward for being in your life

2. A dear friend—someone dear to you

3. A neutral person—a stranger

4. A difficult person—someone you dislike

5. All beings—everyone, everywhere

You can use phrases from a prayer on the Brahma-viharas that relate to sympathetic joy, such as "May all beings never be separated from bliss," or any phrase or series of phrases that wishes joy for others.

TRY THIS

The following sympathetic joy meditation is based on the teachings of IMSB teacher Shaila Catherine. An audio version of it is available for you to download at www.newharbinger.com/27954.

Sit down to meditate, and close your eyes. When you feel grounded and settled, begin this meditation by reflecting on your benefactor's basic goodness: times when this person has acted with honorable qualities, such as openness, equanimity, or compassion; occasions when this person has experienced great happiness; or different ways you feel grateful for what this person has given you.

As you visualize your benefactor, invite your mind to settle and your heart to open so that there's a sense of spaciousness. Repeat and affirm, "May _____ (your benefactor) never be separated from bliss," or any phrase or series of phrases that wishes this person joy. Allow the wish to radiate from you to your benefactor. If you have difficulty wishing success and wellness on a benefactor, you may wish to start with the "dear friend" category.

Once you feel a sense of ease in your practice of sympathetic joy for your benefactor, you may choose to continue and expand to the next category: a dear friend, a neutral person, a difficult person, and finally all beings. As with the loving-kindness practice, this will, most probably, occur over many sittings. Wishing happiness and success to others, particularly a person with whom you're having difficulty, is typically not easy. Recognize when you've gone far enough, and return to your breath to end the meditation or to create a break before you resume sending joy. Over time, as your practice grows stronger, you'll be able to recognize the basic goodness in all and will more easily wish unconditional joy to everyone, without distinction.

43. Taste the Elixir

Our conditioned competitive spirit inclines us toward feelings of jealousy and envy. These and other states, such as judgment, conceit, and prejudice, result from a mind that naturally compares. This "comparing mind" comes from the misperception that the self is something separate from others, reinforced by our constant use of the words "I," "me," and "mine." Holding on to a rigid sense of self maintains this dualistic relationship and keeps you from experiencing the dynamic unfolding of each moment. As long as your comparing mind is at work, you'll never be at ease. There'll always be someone who's "better" than you. Ultimately comparison results in feeling worse or in a happiness that doesn't last.

The practice of sympathetic joy is the elixir for a "comparing mind," because it breaks down the barriers between you and others. The unselfishness of sympathetic joy allows you to step outside yourself. By rejoicing in others' joy, you see the big picture: you recognize the shared sense of vulnerability in being human and the basic goodness within all beings.

Of the four "heavenly abodes" or "heart qualities"—equanimity, compassion, sympathetic joy, and loving-kindness—sympathetic joy is regarded as the most difficult to cultivate. It's not easy to wish your so-called enemies well. But when you have pure intentions for others' success and well-being, your heart opens, and you're able to see your own good fortune.

TRY THIS

Sooner or later, there will be a time when someone you love or care for deeply is able to attend a wonderful event that you're unable to participate in yourself. Perhaps you need to finish a project, have a conflicting obligation, or feel ill. This presents an opportunity to informally practice sympathetic joy. Before the event, ask the other person to take a photo or obtain a memento to share with you afterward. As you regard it, listen to the other person's account, and imagine what he or she experienced. Vicariously feel his or her enjoyment—as if you're soaking in his or her happiness.

Once you're able to feel a sense of ease toward this person, expand this practice to other categories of people who are at events you wish you were at yourself.

44. An Antidote

When feeling deprived in some way, we tend to hold tightly to what we have, because it doesn't feel as if there's enough to go around. But, as Buddha taught, it's this very act of clinging that's the cause of our suffering. To move from a place of scarcity to one of abundance, paradoxically, you let go. You participate in the very practice of letting go: generosity.

Generosity

Generosity, the practice of giving without needing to get anything in return, is considered the most basic way to find freedom from suffering.

In Buddhism, generosity is like a pair of bookends: it's the first practice taught by the Buddha but also considered the highest and most ennobling of his teachings. Generosity is a way of unconditionally caring for others and, in the process, caring for yourself. As you hold yourself in the warmth of compassion, the less there is to hold on to and the more there is to freely give. In Buddhism, *dana* means the practice of giving. You can practice *dana* in tangible ways, such as giving others food, money, or shelter, or in intangible ways, such as giving someone your full attention, love, acceptance, or a smile.

Giving frees you from clinging to wanting yourself and your experiences to be a certain way: holding on to assumptions, expectations, things, and ideas. Generosity creates spaciousness and joy. You may feel a certain "lightness of being" or a breeze of fresh air when you practice generosity.

Thich Nhat Hanh's concept of "interbeing" teaches that we're dependent on one another for our material needs, just as we're dependent on others' kindness. As you shift your orientation from individuality to mutuality and from independence to interdependence, you change not only the way you relate to others, but also the way you relate to yourself.

Through the practice of generosity—of selfless giving—you let go of the barriers that bind and confine you, and you open into a limitless space of being, filled with loving-kindness and joy. There's so much pleasure in giving that you're offering yourself a gift as well.

TRY THIS

For today, practice giving and receiving gifts. You can offer others something tangible, like a present or a nice lunch, or something intangible, like your time, energy, or support. Notice what happens once you've freely given.

Do you feel yourself expand, or do you feel yourself contract? Are there feelings of nobility or joy, or are there feelings of regret or strain? If someone extends a gift to *you*, are you able to graciously accept? Does receiving allow you to feel nourished and blessed, or does it take you out of your comfort zone? How does letting go feel different from holding on? Can you get a reading on your level of suffering and well-being? How does selflessness feel distinct from self-centeredness? Can you feel a greater sense of connection to others and yourself and recognize the basic goodness in all?

PART 4

BEING IN THE WORLD

In this final part of the book, you'll learn to bring the qualities of acceptance and compassion into your actions through living a life of virtue. Living a life of virtue means committing to your deepest values no matter what comes your way. It means caring for yourself and others by being careful to not cause harm through your thoughts, attitudes, speech, or actions. Working mindfully with your thoughts helps you see clearly and respond skillfully. Working compassionately with your emotions provides a sense of your inherent worth and helps you hold to your intention to stay true to your core values. Acting with integrity and wholeness helps you share your inner peace with others and, in doing so, contribute to the happiness of all.

Buddhism teaches three virtue practices. These are practices that grow from within you and manifest in how you relate to and impact others and the world. They're part of the Noble Eightfold Path, or the Path of Awakening—which consists of these three virtue practices, two wisdom practices, and three concentration practices. While the practices are somewhat sequential, they're also simultaneous. Because they're interrelated, they inspire and energize one another. Implicit in each practice is having *right* or *wise* understanding and intention.

The virtue practices focus on ethical conduct and the intention not to cause harm. They comprise *right speech*—interacting with others to not cause harm; *right action*—relating to others without getting caught up in your wants and emotions or judgmental thoughts and views; and *right livelihood*—taking care of yourself by not taking advantage of others.

The word "right" in the names of these practices doesn't mean "correct in a prescribed way." Rather, it entails responding wisely from a clear mind and fearless heart.

45. Claim Your Emotional Baggage

Living a life of virtue starts with inner preparation, or caring for your mind and heart states. This includes understanding what you carve out in yourself as unwanted and how you disown those parts, so that you don't unload them on others.

Not respecting your whole self is like throwing out a guest at your party because she hasn't conformed to the dress code. But when you greet your guests with acceptance and compassion, you don't see just the clothes they wear, you see their whole self and invite them in or allow them to stay.

Caring for Your Mind and Heart States

When you react on autopilot, your actions are typically motivated by not wanting to feel emotional pain. This refers back to resistance to one of the basic truths of existence: *dukkha*, or suffering. As you repeatedly react from this defensive position, you collect emotional baggage along the way.

Emotional baggage may be *a way you disown yourself and deem yourself unacceptable.* For example, perhaps you're particularly sensitive to being corrected. This may stem from a critical parent who was blaming and punitive when you made mistakes or didn't perform to perfection. Now, whenever your husband corrects your speech (which he often does) because you've mispronounced a word, used the wrong word, or relayed faulty information, you feel criticized and inadequate. You express your irritation and blame him for always needing to find fault in what you're saying. Your unfinished issue of inadequacy is being triggered and carried as emotional baggage.

Emotional baggage may also be *a judgment or expectation that limits and defines who you are.* To continue the example above, let's say that your husband is extremely well-informed, knowledgeable, and self-sufficient. While these traits have many advantages, they're also limiting. They keep him from asking for help or getting emotionally closer to others, including you. These attributes might stem from a highly intellectual, emotionally distant family of origin. While focusing on becoming an information gatherer may have offered your husband some sense of connection with his family, it was also a way of protecting against vulnerability and neglect. Since he couldn't depend on his family, he needed to care for himself by building competence and becoming independent. This might be why he feels so compelled to correct your speech. He's trying to shore you up with the same coping mechanism that he used himself: competence. While he's trying to be helpful, he inadvertently fuels your own unresolved issues with inadequacy.

Emotional baggage can also be *internal conflict*. For example, you've decided to go on a diet to lose weight, but you repeatedly sabotage your own efforts. Though your intention is to drop pounds in order to feel better and fit into a size eight dress, you don't like being judged on looks. This conflict might stem from a mother who placed excessive value on outward appearance and little value on inner strengths. The result is that you have issues with control and find yourself caught in cycles of fighting for control and losing control. The longer you carry your emotional baggage, the heavier it becomes. The more pounds you gain!

When you pay close attention to the cause-and-effect relationship between your mind and heart states and your actions, you are better able to free yourself from unwanted feelings and stop their harmful effects. Anxiety, fear, and depression can be powerful emotions, but you don't have to carry them around all the time.

Through wise understanding and compassion, you develop the ability to work with your mind and heart states to not inflict harm. You learn to live in harmony with yourself: resolving internal conflicts, letting go of expectations, and not thinking in terms of good versus bad and right versus wrong. In this way, you're better equipped to help others and create stronger relationships.

Invariably, items get tossed into your emotional baggage, because there's always an endless supply of "objects of *non*-attention." Just remember that no matter how often an undesired item gets thrown in, you can always recognize and see it for what it is: unnecessary baggage. Then you can take it out again.

TRY THIS

Find a little bag, such as a makeup or jewelry bag, and attach a travel identification card to identify it as emotional baggage. This symbolizes your unfinished issues that you carry with you. Every time an unresolved issue emerges—a way you disown yourself and deem yourself unacceptable; a judgment or expectation that limits and defines who you are; or an internal conflict—place a rock inside the bag. Ask yourself:

- *Where do my internal conflicts come from* (for example, a critical, neglectful, or judgmental parent)?

- *What is the pain I want to avoid* (for example, a fear of being inadequate, abandoned, or controlled)?

- *What am I ignoring* (for example, being compassionate, thoughtful, or patient)?

Every time you "make peace, not war"—not react from your emotional baggage—take a rock out of your bag. Notice how much lighter it becomes!

46. Listen—Just Listen

Speech, both oral and written, is so powerful an influence on human relationships and society that Buddha determined it worthy of inclusion on the Noble Eightfold Path! This is the first of the virtue practices, *right speech*: interacting with others to not cause harm. Your interactions with others begin with the silent talk in your head. Emotionally charged or judgmental thoughts lead to emotionally charged or judgmental speech. Any time you feel angry or afraid, before you know it you may be identifying with your feelings and your emotional baggage may be coming out of your mouth. When this happens, sooner or later the situation only gets worse. *What* you have to say, *when* you choose to say it, and *whether* it's actually true are invariably skewed.

One way of causing harm and not living a life of virtue is through blame—putting your efforts into either trying to prove yourself right because you feel guilty or trying to prove others wrong by displacing your emotions onto them. If you have blame to hide behind, your fortress of self-esteem has a thick defensive wall, but an interior that lies in disrepair.

Pema Chödrön explains this constant need to prove yourself right or prove others wrong as a way to solidify yourself in an uncertain or nebulous world. "Everything is ambiguous, everything is always shifting and changing, and there are as many different takes on any given situation as there are people involved. Trying to find absolute rights and wrongs is a trick we play on ourselves to feel secure and comfortable" (Chödrön 2000, 83). What we need to do, Chödrön suggests, is be more compassionate toward all these parts of ourselves.

Blame manifests from ill will, one of the "five hindrances" that Buddhist psychology identifies as leading to unwholesome action. These hindrances are so powerful and seductive, they incline us to lose sight of the big picture and get sidetracked into little dramas that we end up taking out on others. To work with your mind and heart states, you need to understand the forms that these psychological forces can take.

- **Sensual desire** can take the form of compulsive wanting (clinging), such as obsessing over or fantasizing about something or fantasizing about or flirting with someone you can't have.

- **Ill will** manifests as not wanting something (aversion), such as attacking with some type of hostility and pushing your partner away through critical, judgmental, and hurtful behavior.

- **Sloth and torpor** are represented by laziness and boredom, such as losing interest because you're not engaged in activities you can identify with, even though they're important to others, such as what your partner does professionally.

- **Restlessness and worry** comes from wanting things to be different (clinging to pleasure and avoiding pain), like finding ways to distract yourself from your relationship by not being available.

- **Doubt** is characterized by losing faith or becoming disheartened—for example, questioning your commitment to your relationship.

Each of the hindrances has antidotes that neutralize their effect. These include the following:

- **Sensual desire** can be neutralized by devotion to, commitment to, or interest in the one you love.

- **Ill will** can be neutralized by exploring your beliefs and speaking from your heart.

- **Sloth and torpor** can be neutralized by quieting your mind to investigate what you're resisting.

- **Restlessness and worry** can be neutralized by moving into your feelings of discomfort to feel more connected.

- **Doubt** can be neutralized by understanding your loss of faith, such as sadness, jealousy, or inadequacy, and using your strengths to carry you through.

As you come to understand and learn how to work with unwholesome emotions, you can meet an essential condition for right speech: being able to listen—*really* listen. This means listening for the purpose of understanding, not to satisfy your own agenda or prove that you're right. It requires putting yourself in the other person's shoes so that you can step out of yourself and feel what *he or she* is feeling. You do this not by avoiding or ignoring your feelings, but by softening around them: not holding on to them so tightly that you need to attack or defend. Another condition for right speech is being *really* present: paying close attention, withholding judgment, and relating with kindness.

TRY THIS

The following exercise teaches the skill of listening—*really* listening.

With a partner, come up with three or four questions to better understand each other, questions like "What's something you're struggling with?" "What's something you'd like me to understand?" "How do I contribute to this difficulty?" "Tell me, how can I help?" When you have your list of questions, decide who will ask them first. That person asks a single question at a time, and the other person responds. Allow five to ten minutes total response time. Then reverse roles.

It's important that the person asking the questions not comment, analyze, interrogate, defend, or reply in any way to the other person's responses. The intention is to simply listen. It's not uncommon to notice the impulse to speak up and the need to have an impact in some way. Learning to listen and not interrupt, however, allows the other person to deal with disappointment or stress in his or her own way. You legitimize the other person's feelings simply by listening to how he or she is feeling.

After you've reversed roles, take another five to ten minutes in mutual dialogue, sharing your experience. Have you discovered something new about yourself or the other person? Do you have deeper understanding? Is there a greater sense of closeness or empathy?

47. Speak with Compassion

When you criticize, give unsolicited advice, gossip, lie, insult, accuse, or attack, you're engaging in harmful speech. But speech can also be harmful in more subtle ways—for example, when you interrupt, dominate, or manipulate, or when you fill the air with empty talk. Unfortunately, we give and receive harmful speech so often that we're mostly oblivious to it.

Caring for Your Relationships

In his book *Dancing with Life*, Insight meditation teacher Phillip Moffitt writes: "The practice of right speech is built around meeting three conditions simultaneously: Say only what is *true* and *useful* and *timely*. If any one of these criteria isn't met, then *silence* is the wise form of speech. This is such a simple formula and easy to recall even in moments of strong emotion, but it's very hard to execute even under the best of conditions because the grasping mind corrupts speech faster than it does action"

(Moffitt 2012, 240). Because right speech requires such awareness and compassion, it's considered an advanced practice!

When your speech is true, useful, and timely, it's intentional, thoughtful, and effective. With right speech comes greater empathy, sensitivity, and awareness. The more you practice right speech, the more you're able to respond from a place of mindful self-esteem.

TRY THIS

A relationship-building exercise that's a good follow-up to paired listening is called *active listening.* One person (the speaker) says something important for the other person (the listener) to understand. This might refer back to an issue made known in the paired listening exercise or to a disagreement, misunderstanding, or concern. The listener focuses on just listening and then repeats what was heard, without interpreting, defending, correcting, or offering advice. If the speaker feels only partially understood, the speaker first acknowledges what was correct and then clarifies what needs greater understanding, being careful not to add anything new. The listener then, again, repeats what was heard. This half of the exercise is complete when the speaker feels fully understood. Then reverse roles.

There's no prescribed time limit for this exercise. However, you might want to decide in advance the maximum amount of time you're able to devote to it. This exercise is difficult for most partners or close friends, and it often takes several tries to reach true understandings. Don't worry if it takes you many attempts.

Tips:

- When you're the speaker, it's important to deliver your message clearly and concisely. Often, our spoken messages are too long and vague. We're too tempted to take the opportunity to place blame and include all the ways we feel defeated, unappreciated, or ignored. There's also the desire to really make the point by speaking in extremes: "You *always* do this"; "You *never* do that!" When you speak like this, it's no wonder that your partner defends, checks out, or attacks—in other words, doesn't listen! So try to avoid it.

- When you're the listener, it's not uncommon to feel impatient. It takes time to truly listen, time during which you may feel uncomfortable that you're not "doing" anything. In addition, all too often, the need to be right surpasses the need to get along, making listening an even greater challenge. Be mindful of the urge to speak up, but let it pass.

Afterward, take some time to share what this experience was like. What did it feel like to be really heard and understood, and what did it feel like to really listen and understand? Notice what feelings emerged. Did your emotions soften? Did your heart open?

48. Practice Nonharming

Second on the list of virtue practices is *right action*: acting without causing harm to yourself or others by means of judgmental thoughts and emotional needs. Through the practice of right action, you see how unwholesome actions lead to unsound states of mind. When you see the cause-and-effect relationship between your actions and your mind states, you see your reflection. You see your suffering when you're wrapped in greed, jealousy, or resentment, and you see your happiness when you're imbued with generosity, kindness, or patience. It's empowering to recognize that you're not dependent on others changing (which you have no control over anyway) and that you're the source of your own happiness. While interpersonal dynamics are a 50/50 operation, you take 100 percent responsibility for your share of the action.

Buddha spoke of five precepts to living a life of right action. Living according to these guiding principles has the capacity to be life changing:

1. Refrain from harming, especially from taking life. Cultivate respect for life; honor and protect all living things.

2. Refrain from stealing and from taking what's not given, including being exploitative, dishonest, and deceptive. Cultivate generosity; give your time and resources for the justice and well-being of all.

3. Refrain from misbehaving sexually. Cultivate kindness and honesty; be sensitive, and honor your commitments.

4. Refrain from causing harm through speech. Cultivate understanding; listen deeply, and speak wisely.

5. Refrain from indulging in intoxicants, including unhealthy food and entertainment. Cultivate self-care; protect your health and wellness.

When you make the choice to not cause suffering, you commit to repeatedly asking yourself, *Am I causing suffering, or am I causing non-suffering?* In other words, how are you treating yourself and others? Are your motivations driven by a need to get versus give; manipulate versus care for; seek approval versus bring happiness; rush toward the goal versus engage in the process; or ignore your needs versus nourish yourself?

Be guided by your values. Show what you care about through your actions. If you care about your health, exercise regularly. If you care about your partner, express your love often. If you care about the planet, do what you can, in small or large measure, to not contribute to climate change. There's always choice in what you say and what you do.

Because we're all connected to one another, our words and actions travel far and wide. When you're flying as a kite in the canyon of Mother Earth, listen for the echo of your words; look for the silhouette of your actions.

TRY THIS

Practice right action throughout the day with the intention of not causing harm to yourself or others. Repeatedly ask yourself, *Am I causing suffering, or am I causing nonsuffering?* Practicing nonharming may include speaking kindly, supporting a colleague at work, slowing down when you need to rest, volunteering at the humane society, or working for a cause you believe in.

Notice how the wisdom practices of *right view* (observing, reflecting on, and understanding what is being experienced) and *right intention* (responding to life mindfully and compassionately) and the concentration practices of *right effort* (paying attention and shifting your attention wisely), *right mindfulness* (being fully present in order to see clearly and respond skillfully), and *right concentration* (having a mind that's focused and able to be present) influence your actions.

- Right intention: Do your actions match with your core values?

- Right view: Are you using observation to understand?

- Right effort: Are you applying and maintaining your effort wisely?

- Right mindfulness: Are you staying in the present to see clearly and respond wisely?

- Right concentration: Is your mind steady?

As you bring awareness to how you interface with the world, how do you experience yourself? If externally driven self-esteem in which "practice is to make perfect" is at one end of a continuum, and internally based self-esteem wherein "perfect is the practice" is at the other, where are you on this continuum?

49. Write Your Job Description

The last of the three virtue practices is *right livelihood*: engaging in work with the intention of not causing harm to yourself or others—acting with truth and integrity without trying to take advantage of or manipulate others. Buddha offered teachings on prosperity at home, at work, and in the world (Rahula 2008) and advised that we "gradually increase wealth without squeezing others, just as bees collect honey without harming flowers" (Rahula 2008, 15).

Success in the workplace comes from more than hard work. It starts with removing self-imposed barriers and trusting in your own potential to be self-reliant. It requires *right effort*: making wise decisions and taking wise actions. This includes developing the necessary knowledge and skills, being organized, being timely, and thinking "outside of the box" (Rahula 2008, 21–25).

There are many personal and interpersonal, immediate and distant consequences of what we do to earn a living. Ethical conduct and intention in your work means being aware of the choices you make and the impact these choices have on you, others, and the world. It's not so much what you get, but what you give.

In the illuminating book *Insight Meditation: The Practice of Freedom*, renowned mindfulness teacher Joseph Goldstein suggests infusing whatever job you do with a "spirit of service" that can take you far in your practice of freedom. He offers a beautiful quote from the Dalai Lama: "We are visitors on this planet. We are here for ninety, a hundred years at the very most. During that period we must try to do something good, something useful with our lives. Try to be at peace with yourself and help others share that peace. If you contribute to other people's happiness, you will find the true goal, the true meaning of life" (Goldstein 1993, 160).

TRY THIS

Explore how your work can become more meaningful. How can it be better aligned with your values and beliefs? Through your work, how can you deepen your awareness and extend your kindness to others? If you were to write a set of guidelines on how to work from a "spirit of service," what would it say? How would it honor your strengths and be a source of joy? Put down your thoughts in a journal entry titled "Job Description."

50. Life Is the Practice

As you're guided by the virtue practices and the intention of not inflicting harm, you learn to take responsibility for your thoughts, attitudes, and actions; let go of your emotional baggage; choose how to respond skillfully; pay attention to what really matters; and hold to the truth of your Buddha nature.

Caring for the World

Because of our inherent commonality and our utter interdependence as humans, you journey on the Path of Awakening not just for yourself but for the benefit of all (Goldstein 1993, 170). Understanding this truth changes how you relate to others. Practicing this truth recognizes your basic goodness and the basic goodness in all.

When your self-esteem honors interdependence and you take responsibility for the well-being of all, you engage in acts of selflessness. With virtue as your guide, you pay reverence to the whole of life—tending to yourself, others, and the world with the guiding light of what's truly important. *Life* is the practice.

Living a virtuous life means bringing an integrated awareness of your mind and heart states into action, whether at work or at play—in the day or at night. You replace your autopilot with an awareness of living life fully, in harmonious flow, for the good of all. This is the transformation from living life as a separate, small self to a big self who's part of a far greater reality.

Jack Kornfield, one of the leading Buddhist teachers in the West, says: "To awaken to this mysterious grandeur that we, in life, are a part of, allows us to step out of our limited identity and have it connected with something that is greater, and then the two inform one another. It's not that you lose yourself, but in some way, you are free— more to be your unique beautiful self because you are not so frightened anymore. You feel that you are a part of the whole" (Kornfield 2012).

May you live your life from the virtuous intention of this ancient Sanskrit chant: "May all beings everywhere be happy and free, and may the thoughts, words, and actions of our own life contribute in some way to that happiness and that freedom for all."

TRY THIS

For the following guided visualization, settle into a comfortable position and gently close your eyes. Allow your breath to find its own rhythm. As your mind relaxes and a feeling of calm presides, imagine walking into an open meadow, one that's surrounded by pine trees and covered in wildflowers. While wandering in this magical place, you come upon a small, clear pond. You stop to sit on a smooth rock overlooking the pond, to take in its beauty. To your wonderment, as you gaze into the pond, you see the image of Buddha or someone else who's filled with right wisdom, right virtue, and right concentration.

Keep looking at this vision until the identity of this awakened person becomes clear. Like the sun's indiscriminate warming rays, the presence of this being contributes to the happiness of all. As you deeply look upon this person, you see a mind that's open, aware, and wise; a heart filled with loving-kindness and compassion; and a life lived in virtue. With each breath, you take in more and more of the brilliance that radiates from this person.

As the vision of this embodiment of the Eightfold Path slowly dissolves, imagine gently rising to stand on the rock and bowing to the vision in the pond. Take the lasting presence of the person in your vision with you.

EPILOGUE

With the wakefulness of mindfulness, you become aware of how acceptance allows you to expand, while fear and insecurity cause you to contract. You acknowledge the futility of resisting the changing nature of the waves and currents of your mind. With the warmth of compassion, you soften your heart and relax into the fearless knowing of your whole self: your perfection within your imperfection. You don't push against the tide to become anyone other than who you already are.

With the wisdom that comes from living a life of virtue, you honor yourself enough to know you're not the center of the universe, and you chart your course by the North Star. You commit to caring for others as you pledge to care for yourself and contribute to happiness on land and at sea. You meet the world with an awakened mind, a compassionate heart, and a helping hand.

You accept the surge of dissatisfaction (*dukkha*) as inevitable; you accept change (*anicca*) as constant; and you accept that a permanent, static self is an illusion (*anatta*). You ride between the waves of effort and surrender—making intentional endeavors while simultaneously letting go into life's dynamic flow. You relinquish following the course that leads from point A to point B and rather move toward yourself, starting where you are, and authentically moving from there—in the constant ebb and flow of the ocean tides.

You come to know yourself not as the wave that fluctuates—sometimes big, sometimes little—with the slightest wind, but as the vast, limitless ocean that contains all things. You begin to have a sense of wholeness, a sense that you're "enough."

When you look at the night sky to get your bearings, you don't lose its wholeness as you look at the different constellations. You don't try to gain a sense of security by creating a fixed, solid concept of "self" to compare against others, limiting your view and shielding you from seeing your inherent goodness. You know that you're part of the greater whole; there's no sense of scarcity in the midst of abundance. There's no lone star outside the infinite universe.

You must ask yourself: *Who am I, really? What belongs to me? What do I really need to protect and defend? Is it true that I never measure up—that what I do is never good enough? What is this endless pursuit of self-esteem?*

This is a long journey, the journey of a lifetime. It's indeed a curious ship that sails into the mystery with nothing on board save confidence of mind, courage of heart, and commitment of purpose. This is the journey of mindful self-esteem that unfolds and arises from the qualities of acceptance, compassion, and a virtuous life.

Continue Your Journey

Let your heart lead you to your quiet place. Sit relaxed and alert, with your eyes closed. Enter into the present moment by anchoring yourself to your breath, grounding yourself in your body, and quieting your mind. With a spacious and open heart, rest your awareness in the precious moment. Savor the stillness. In this silent space, ask yourself, *What brought me here?* Explore the deep motivation, the intention that led you to this book. Acknowledge any degree of confidence, courage, or commitment that furthered you on this journey. Bow to whatever qualities you cultivated that led you to the qualities of mindful self-esteem.

Whenever you're ready, slowly and gently open your eyes.

RESOURCES

Mark Abramson—Stanford Center for Integrative Medicine
stanfordhospital.org/clinicsmedServices/clinics/complementaryMedicine

Renée Burgard
mindfulnesshealth.com

Tara Brach—Insight Meditation Community of Washington, Bethesda, MD
imcw.org

Shaila Catherine—Insight Meditation South Bay, Mountain View, CA
imsb.org

Pema Chödrön—Gampo Abbey, Pleasant Bay, Nova Scotia, Canada
gampoabbey.org

Steve Flowers
mindfullivingprograms.com

Gil Fronsdal—Insight Meditation Center, Redwood City, CA
insightmeditationcenter.org

Christopher Germer
mindfulselfcompassion.org

Joseph Goldstein, Sharon Salzberg—Insight Meditation Society, Barre, MA
dharma.org

Jon Kabat-Zinn, Saki Santorelli—Center for Mindfulness at University of Massachusetts Medical School
umassmed.edu/cfm

Janetti Marotta
janettimarotta.com

Kristin Neff
self-compassion.org

Thich Nhat Hanh—Plum Village, Dordogne, France
plumvillage.org

Daniel Siegel
mindsightinstitute.com

Bob Stahl
mindfulnessprograms.com
insightsantacruz.org

REFERENCES

Bhikkhu, B. 2012. *The Numerical Discourses of the Buddha: A Translation of the Anguttara Nikaya.* Somerville, MA: Wisdom Publications.

Bodhipaksa. 2009. "Dealing with Resistance to Meditation." Wildmind. http://www.wildmind.org/applied/daily-life/dealing-with-resistance.

Boorstein, S. 1996. *Don't Just Do Something, Sit There: A Mindfulness Retreat.* New York: Harper Collins Publishers.

Boyd, J. 1975. *Satan and Mara: Christian and Buddhist Symbols of Evil.* Leiden, The Netherlands: E. J. Brill.

Brach, T. 2012. *True Refuge: Finding Peace and Freedom in Your Own Awakened Heart.* New York: Random House.

Burns, D. 1980. *Feeling Good: The New Mood Therapy.* New York: Avon Books.

Catherine, S. 2008. *Focused and Fearless: A Meditator's Guide to States of Deep Joy, Calm, and Clarity.* Somerville, MA: Wisdom Publications.

Chödrön, P. 2000. *When Things Fall Apart: Heart Advice for Difficult Times.* Boston: Shambhala.

Emmons, R. 2007. *Thanks! How the New Science of Gratitude Can Make You Happier.* New York: Houghton Mifflin.

Fronsdal, G. 2001. *The Issue at Hand: Essays on Buddhist Mindfulness Practice*. Redwood City, CA: Insight Meditation Center.

———. 2008, Oct. 29. Introduction to Mindfulness Meditation series. Insight Meditation Center, Redwood City, CA. Transcript of talk available at http://www.insightmeditation center.org/books-articles/articles/introduction-to-meditation -transcripts/5/.

Germer, C. 2009. *The Mindful Path to Self-Compassion: Freeing Yourself from Destructive Thoughts and Emotions*. New York: Guilford Press.

Germer, C., R. Siegel, and P. Fulton. 2005. *Mindfulness and Psychotherapy*. New York: Guilford Press.

Goldstein, J. 1993. *Insight Meditation: The Practice of Freedom*. Boston: Shambhala.

Hanson, R. 2009. *Buddha's Brain: The Practical Neuroscience of Happiness, Love, and Wisdom*. Oakland, CA: New Harbinger Publications.

Hayes, S. 2008. *Get Out of Your Mind and Into Your Life*. With S. Smith. Oakland, CA: New Harbinger Publications.

Kabat-Zinn, J. 1990. *Full Catastrophe Living: Using the Wisdom of Your Body and Mind to Face Stress, Pain, and Illness*. New York: Dell.

Kaplan, R. 1999. *The Nothing That Is: A Natural History of Zero*. New York: Oxford University Press.

Katie, B. 2002. *Loving What Is: Four Questions That Can Change Your Life*. With S. Mitchell. New York: Harmony Books.

Kornfield, J. 2008. *The Wise Heart: A Guide to the Universal Teachings of Buddhist Psychology*. New York: Bantam Books.

———. 2012, Oct. 26. *Helping Clients Find Their Wise Hearts* (tele-seminar). National Institute for the Clinical Application of Behavioral Medicine (NICABM), Program on Mindfulness, Mansfield Center, CT.

Kung, C. 2006. *Heart of a Buddha.* Taiwan: Amitabha Publications.

Lao-tzu. 1944. *The Way of Life According to Laotzu.* Translated by W. Bynner. New York: John Day. Reprint, New York: Penguin Putnam, 1986.

———. 1988. *Tao Te Ching.* Translated by S. Mitchell. New York: Harper Collins.

Levine, S. 1979. *A Gradual Awakening.* New York: Anchor Books.

Mitchell, S. 2009. *The Second Book of the Tao.* New York: Penguin Press.

Moffitt, P. 2002. "Selfless Gratitude." *Yoga Journal* 168: 61–66.

———. 2012. *Dancing with Life: Buddhist Insights for Finding Meaning and Joy in the Face of Suffering.* New York: Rodale.

Neff, K. 2011. *Self-Compassion: Stop Beating Yourself Up and Leave Insecurity Behind.* New York: Harper Collins.

Neff, K., S. Rude, and K. Kirkpatrick. 2007. "An Examination of Self-Compassion in Relation to Positive Psychological Functioning and Personality Traits." *Journal of Research in Personality* 41: 908–16.

Nhat Hanh, T. 1976. *The Miracle of Mindfulness: An Introduction to the Practice of Meditation.* Boston: Beacon Press.

———. 1992. *Peace Is Every Step: The Path of Mindfulness in Everyday Life.* New York: Bantam Books.

Peterson, C. 2012, Sept. 13. "Smiling and Stress." *The Good Life* (blog), *Psychology Today.* http://www.psychologytoday.com/blog/the-good-life/201209/smiling-and-stress.

Rahula, B. 2008. *The Buddha's Teachings on Prosperity: At Home, at Work, and in the World.* Boston: Wisdom Publications.

Roshi, S. 1986. *Zen Mind, Beginner's Mind.* New York: Weatherhill.

Salzberg, S. 2002. *Lovingkindness: The Revolutionary Art of Happiness.* Boston: Shambhala.

Sendak, M. 1963. *Where the Wild Things Are*. New York: Harper Collins.

Siegel, D. 2010. *Mindsight: The New Science of Personal Transformation*. New York: Bantam Books.

Stahl, B., and E. Goldstein. 2010. *A Mindfulness-Based Stress Reduction Workbook*. Oakland, CA: New Harbinger Publications.

The Union for Reform Judaism—Department of Lifelong Learning and URJ Press. 2004, Nov. 4. "Ethical Teachings—Selections from Pirkei Avot." 10 Minutes of Torah—Jewish Ethics. http://tmt.urj.net/archives/4jewishethics/110404.htm.

Ware, B. 2012. *The Top Five Regrets of the Dying: A Life Transformed by the Dearly Departing*. Australia: Hay House.

Weiss, J. 1986. "Theory and Clinical Observations." In *The Psychoanalytic Process: Theory, Clinical Observation, and Empirical Research*, edited by J. Weiss, H. Sampson, and the Mount Zion Psychotherapy Research Group. New York: Guilford Press.

Weselake, E. 2004. "The Breath of Life." *Yoga Journal* 179: 156.

Young, E. 2002. *Seven Blind Mice*. New York: Puffin Books.

Young, S. 2004. *Break Through Pain: A Step-by-Step Mindfulness Program for Transforming Chronic and Acute Pain*. Boulder, CO: Sounds True.

Zak, P. 2008, Nov. 10. "The Oxytocin Cure." *The Moral Molecule: Neuroscience and Economic Behavior* (blog), *Psychology Today*. http://www.psychologytoday.com/blog/the-moral-molecule/200811/the-oxytocin-cure.

Janetti Marotta, PhD, is a psychologist and coordinator of the mind-body program at Fertility Physicians of Northern California, where she founded the mindfulness-based fertility stress reduction program. She has served on the medical staff of Stanford University Medical Center and treats issues of self-worth as they relate to the broad spectrum of life challenges. She is a longtime practitioner of meditation and mindfulness.

Register your **new harbinger** titles for additional benefits!

When you register your **new harbinger** title—purchased in any format, from any source—you get access to benefits like the following:

- Downloadable accessories like printable worksheets and extra content

- Instructional videos and audio files

- Information about updates, corrections, and new editions

Not every title has accessories, but we're adding new material all the time.

Access free accessories in 3 easy steps:

1. Sign in at NewHarbinger.com (or **register** to create an account).

2. Click on **register a book**. Search for your title and click the **register** button when it appears.

3. Click on the **book cover or title** to go to its details page. Click on **accessories** to view and access files.

That's all there is to it!

If you need help, visit:

NewHarbinger.com/accessories

new harbinger
CELEBRATING
40 YEARS